P9-AFR-039

WHEN PLANETS COLLIDE

A Dating Guide

Jenifer Rose

and

Jim Ghiglieri

Copyright © 2010 by Jenifer Rose and Jim Ghiglieri.

Library of Congress Control Number:		2010908093
ISBN:	Hardcover	978-1-4535-1347-7
	Softcover	978-1-4535-1346-0
	Ebook	978-1-4535-1348-4

All rights reserved. No part of this book may be reproduced or transmitted in any form or by any means, electronic or mechanical, including photocopying, recording, or by any information storage and retrieval system, without permission in writing from the copyright owner.

Cover Art by Janice Baker

This book was printed in the United States of America.

To order additional copies of this book, contact:
info@whenplanetscollide.com or visit: www.whenplanetscollide.com
Xlibris Corporation
1-888-795-4274
www.Xlibris.com
Orders@Xlibris.com
79951

Acknowledgments

Jim

Special thanks to my friends Lonny Dill and Jose Arraiz for their unrelenting insistence that I needed to write a book on dating and share my experience with others. To my mother, Sheri Friberg, for her unwavering support in all aspects of my life. Thank you to Lynn Peterson, Zoe Atcheson, Traci Sessions, and Alicia Herz for their friendship, information, and editing assistance. Mostly to Jenifer Rose, for without her, this book would never have been possible. I think you're the cat's pajamas!

Jen

A very special thanks to Erin Zundel for helping us with the title of the book and to Janice Baker for the design of the book cover. Thank you to Susan Stolte, Erin Zundel, and Christy Freeman. Without the tireless support of these three women, I would never have been able to run a business, host a weekly TV and radio show, and complete this book. Thank you to all three of my children as every time I take on a new project, it takes time away from you. I truly appreciate your understanding and support in everything I do. I absolutely need to thank every client I have ever had at It's Just Lunch as all my knowledge has come from you. In all honesty, I have to thank Jim the most. Thank you for asking me to be your coauthor, thank you for believing in my knowledge and ability, and thank you so much for being relentless and patient enough to push me to the finish line.

Contents

Introduction

Inside these pages, you will find a great many topics that daters currently run into and my advice and then Jenifer's take on the subject. If you don't see the subject matter divided between Jenifer and myself, then we agree on what is written. I don't offer any rebuttals to her opinions as I am not trying to convince her to see my point of view. Rather, I am exposing you to two different trains of thought. The book is about you, with the goal being to offer our expert opinions in a short easy-to-read format. We believe that under this format, someone can pick up the book, flip it to any page, and gather a pearl of dating wisdom or, if they choose, sit down and read the whole thing from cover to cover. The book is intended as a unisex guide, but there are topics directed specifically toward one sex.

This book is directed toward the person seeking advice on dating or, more importantly, catching the right mate and releasing the rest. This is not intended as a relationship book; however, it is difficult to discuss dating and not go into some relational issues. We are not relationship counselors, so what we have to say about maintaining a relationship is based on our experiences and should be taken with a grain of salt.

You may not like what we have to say, but then again, you probably don't like it when someone tells you that you've been doing things wrongly or when their opinions differ from your natural instincts.

Listen up people. If you're reading this, then you're looking for some guidance, and inside these chapters, you'll find tidbits of insight from our years of experience. Our experiences will not mirror your own, but odds are that we have been in the game longer, with more experience, so consider what you read seriously and change your behaviors when and if required. The experiences were not always pleasant, but this book is for you; and we will share the good, the bad, and the ugly (hopefully not too much ugly). So when you read our opinions and we tell you things you should not do, it's likely I did them first or Jenifer interviewed someone who did, and we are trying to save you some of the embarrassment of our past experiences.

Jenifer is a professional matchmaker with years of experience and thousands of predate and postdate interviews. So although our opinions may differ, it doesn't mean one is wrong and the other is right; it simply means that we have our own experiences. We have provided both opinions for you to decide what works for you because ultimately, it is you that will put this information to the test.

This book is not about Jenifer or me; it's about you, understanding and getting what you really want. The contents of the book should be considered as guidelines rather than steadfast rules. You and only you can decide what works at any given moment in time, so skip the ones that don't work for your situation.

Remember the saying "Don't hate the player, hate the game." It was coined by people that are in the game and probably playing well. However, many people can't seem to ever make it to the playing field, so read this book, follow the guidelines and get into the game. Stop standing on the sidelines looking in, be a player not a spectator. The following pages are your playbook, so get on the field, know what you want, and don't give up until you reach your goal.

Getting into the Game

How Many Single People Are out There?

According to the U.S. Census Bureau these are the numbers as of 2005:

89.8 Million
Number of unmarried and single Americans in 2005. This group comprised 41 percent of all U.S. residents age 18 and older.

54%
Percentage of unmarried and single Americans who are women.

60%
Percentage of unmarried and single Americans who have never been married. Another 25 percent are divorced and 15 percent are widowed.

14.9 Million
Number of unmarried and single Americans age 65 and older. These older Americans comprise 14 percent of all unmarried and single people.

86
Number of unmarried men age 18 and older for every 100 unmarried women in the United States.

As you can see, these numbers are strictly for the United States, but when you project them worldwide, the number of singles out there is staggering. According to the U.S. and World Population Clocks, the U.S. population alone is over 308 million, with the world population rapidly approaching 7 billion. That's right. It says 7,000,000,000. Using the 41 percent single people statistics from the U.S. Census Bureau and projecting them worldwide, the number of people over 18 years of age is 2,870,000,000. So when you begin feeling that there are not any single people, guess **again.**

What it really comes down to is that there is no shortage of singles in the United States or worldwide for that matter. So if you're feeling as if there just aren't that many singles, **maybe you need to open your eyes and consider that they** are around you all the time—at the grocery store, the airport, the mall, in traffic, etc. The only time you're not surrounded by them is when you're tucked away at home.

*   *   *

What Do You Want?

Jim

Many people think they want the ideal marriage that society and culture has dictated to them, so that's what they think their life should be. When they achieve what was understood to be the perfect relationship, they find **disappointment and still have the void they sought to fill.** Know the difference between what you think you want and what you really desire at this point in your life. How can you achieve what you really want if you're not sure what it is? Make a list, use it as a guideline, and reference it when necessary.

Jenifer

Lots of people have an idea in their head of what they think the perfect partner would be. In my profession, I have matched people with exactly what they ask for, and they come back only to say, "You gave me exactly what I asked for, and it doesn't work for me." I suggest you date enough to find out what works for you before choosing your next partner. What you want doesn't always work for you. Go out and meet enough people to find out what works for you, and then you can get what you really want.

*   *   *

Know the difference between what you think you want and what you really desire.

Addressing What You Honestly Want

Jim

If you think the house with the white picket fence, 2.3 children, the PTA and a minivan are what you really want **but find yourself daydreaming about your true desire** to have encounters with beautiful women that float in and out of your life, then it's time to reevaluate your real intentions. Be honest with yourself. If you want multiple partners and all that goes with them over the marriage that you thought you wanted, make a change or accept the situation. You should also understand that it works both ways. This is not about telling people to get divorced but that everyone should get exactly what they desire in life, and if you're settling just to get through, then you need to stand up for what you really want and find a way to make it happen. If you're unhappily married, then do something about it. If you want to be married and still pick up on women, then read another book because you're an a—hole.

Jenifer

Many people have a hard time saying out loud what they really want. Why? They feel like it makes them shallow or a bad person if they exclude certain people in the criteria they are trying to set. Every person out in the world has had different life experiences. These experiences have made them feel a certain way about things. This does not make you shallow or bad. It is important to identify why you feel the way you feel about certain things just to make sure it's legitimate. Example: Let's say you've identified the fact that you don't want to date someone who smokes. Ask yourself why. Maybe it's because you're afraid you may start smoking if you spend time around someone who smokes. It could be that you are concerned about the health issues, or you think it will be a bad influence on your children. It doesn't really matter why you feel strongly about it, but it will be helpful if you identify the reasons for your feelings. Example 2: You have decided you don't want to date women of a different ethnic group. You determine that the reason is because you dated one once, and she wasn't a very nice person. Well, I'm pretty sure you can find women in your own ethnic group that are not very nice either. If this is the only reason you can come up with for excluding other ethnic groups, you may want to reconsider.

*   *   *

Expect Rejection

Jim

Face it, you will be rejected; it will not be pleasant, and you will not like it, but it is a fact of life that we all face rejection. When you've learned not to let the rejection bother you, then you'll find it easier to ask women out, and eventually you will hear a yes that makes all those no's seem to disappear. Remember that a shot not taken is always a shot missed, so get out there and take those shots, and don't take it personally if the shot's rejected.

Jenifer

I'm not sure I agree with this topic. Just because someone chooses not to go out with you doesn't make it a personal rejection. You never know what the other person's reasons for making that decision are. Don't read too much into it. Every person isn't right for every other person. Just because they decided you weren't right for them doesn't mean you're not a great person and, quite possibly, the perfect person for someone else. I suppose, technically, if you ask a person out on a date and they don't accept your invitation, they rejected it, but I don't view this as a personal rejection. This is simply a rejection to an invitation, and there could be a multitude of reasons behind it. We certainly don't accept every party or wedding invitation that we receive, and our friends don't feel rejected when we decline.

Negotiables

Jim

There are two lists—negotiable and nonnegotiable—and
they sum up what character traits one can and cannot
accept, and you should have your list too. To give you
an example, poor hygiene, smoking, illegal drug use,
and obesity are areas many people don't want in their
life or the life of those they may date. These go under
the heading of nonnegotiable, and the instant you
find out someone you're dating has a trait listed under
nonnegotiable, then end it no matter how hot you think
they are. On occasion, the person wants to know why
and when you tell them; they either get angry or offer
to change. You should have no desire to change anyone,
so it's over. However, there are many more traits that
are negotiable, and they may be something like religion,
political views, family issues, etc. The ones that fall under
this heading you are willing to work with, if you believe
they won't be a deal breaker somewhere down the
road. Now this works both ways, and you should expect
someone you're interested in to have their own lists, so be
aware that, at some point, they may walk away, and you
may never know why. Accept it and let it go.

Jenifer

I refer to these as preferences and deal breakers. I believe people have several levels of preferences—slight preferences to strong preferences and then absolute deal breakers. Be honest about what your deal breakers are and choose them wisely because you should never start a relationship with someone who has one of your deal breakers. The relationship will eventually end, and someone or possibly both of you will get hurt. Not to mention that starting long term relationships that probably won't last is simply a waste of time. I would like to repeat the fact that you should choose your deal breakers wisely. There are many people out there who have started to date someone with one of the so-called deal breakers, and they ended up together and very happy. This would indicate that it was a strong preference, not really a deal breaker. A good example of a true deal breaker would be if one person feels very strongly about having children and the other person feels very strong about not having children. Someone is going to have to make a huge compromise at some point, and they're most likely going to be very unhappy in the long term. You may want to list this as a deal breaker to make sure you never get in the situation of having to make such a big compromise or of asking someone else to. Addressing what you really want first will help you make an accurate list.

*   *   *

The Ego

Jim

This part of a man can change from bold and brash to timid and unsure in a matter of minutes. When your ego becomes too big, you're considered full of yourself and tend to drive people away from you. The ego that's timid and unsure will certainly drive women away as they see it as almost childlike, creating a situation such that if they enter into a relationship with you, they might as well be raising a child. Few women are interested in having a relationship with a man that acts like their child, so keep your ego in check. There will be times when you feel as though you can conquer the world and times when a woman isn't interested in getting to know you, bruising your fragile ego. So when you feel like you're the king of the world, don't act like it, and when your ego has been bashed, get up dust yourself off and get back in the game.

Jenifer

After conducting over one thousand interviews, I can honestly say that this ego thing is really important. They say they want someone with a strong personality, but also has a sensitive side. There is a fine line on these things, and it can often be confusing. Maybe this is why men always claim they don't know what women want. In regard to women wanting a man with a strong personality, women like to feel safe, and we consider our men as protectors. When a man is timid and unsure, we have a hard time viewing him as our protector. At the same time, we appreciate a sensitive and tender side to a man. The sensitive side is what helps the man identify with the women's feelings and views. The tender side is what makes us feel loved. It is imperative that you find a good balance between these things.

*   *   *

When you are unwilling to compromise with your partner, the dynamics change from a mutual relationship to a dictatorship.

When you initially meet someone, communicate your interests, hobbies, background, and family life as they really are.

Communication and Compromise

Jim

When you refuse to compromise and are reluctant to communicate, you are setting the course of your life in the direction of growing old alone. Relationships are based largely on communication and the ability to discuss the situations that present themselves in your life. One of the biggest complaints that women have is that most men are terrible communicators, so if this is you, consider taking a class on communicating and improving your skills. Being unable to compromise, on the other hand, usually involves selfishness. When you are unwilling to compromise with your partner, the dynamics change from a mutual relationship to a dictatorship. Few people in this world would desire living under your rule, so stop being stubborn and selfish and be willing to compromise. However, there will be times when you feel the need to be steadfast in your decision, but choose these battles wisely as you may be expected to compromise on the next big decision.

Jenifer

When you initially meet someone, communicate your interests, hobbies, background, and family life as they really are. Don't try to be what you think the other person is looking for. This is a waste of time and sets you up to be in another failed relationship. Think through what you're willing to compromise on and what you are not and communicate these things honestly as well. As your relationship progresses, the communication will become very important, so treat it as such. Again, make sure you are being completely honest in your communication. At the end of each date, you will both be deciding if you want to go out again. This decision needs to be based on honest communication so the relationship can have a lasting chance.

*   *   *

To be great at dating, you must be a great conversationalist.

Meeting Versus Date

Jim

This applies primarily to meeting people on the Internet; however, it includes dating services and blind dates. When meeting someone for the first time, it's really more like an interview, where you use the time together to decide if you would actually like to go out on a date. When meeting someone for the first time, you should be prepared with questions that are relevant to what you're really seeking in your life, and for god's sake, be on time. If you have a profile to view, then take notes on that to help formulate your inquiries. A date, on the other hand, comes after you have already met face-to-face and mutually decided that you would like to spend more time together and see where it leads.

Jenifer

It is incredibly important that on the first introduction (meeting), you keep things very light and fun. To be great at dating, you must be a great conversationalist. You never want the first meeting to come across as an interrogation, so while I agree you should have an idea of some questions and things you want to learn at the first meeting, remember to be interested and interesting.

Make sure you come across as friendly and conversational so it won't seem like an interrogation. In an effort to keep things light and fun, never talk about things that are heavy or negative. Some examples would be your nasty divorce, your crazy ex, illnesses, etc. Talk only about the positive things in your life, and make an effort to find out what the two of you have in common and what your views on life are. Take the time to learn about their profession and their family life as well. These things will give you enough information to decide if you want to ask them out on a date.

*   *   *

Long-Distance Dating

This can have tremendous benefits depending on what you are truly seeking. If you're interested in being with someone occasionally and both have a no-strings-attached attitude, it can be great fun and allow both of you the freedoms you desire. However, many times one person becomes attached, and it gets more complicated. If this happens, you need to mutually decide in which direction you would both like things to go, and if you're not in agreement, then end it before someone gets hurt and find exactly what you seek.

*   *   *

Long-Distance Relationships

Jim

OK, so you've done the long-distance dating thing and decided to go forward into a genuine relationship. Consider that eventually one of you will have to move for it to work, and whoever it is will experience life-altering changes. Don't rush into this blindly as one of you will be turning their life upside down. In the interim, while you're trying to do what is necessary to maintain the relationship, arguments will arise, usually over not seeing each other enough. These arguments boil down to one person that's not willing or is unable to travel for a visit. If this lasts for three or four weeks, things will deteriorate rapidly, and the relationship can unravel. When entering into this type of relationship, understand that you may need to travel even when you don't feel you have the time or inclination. It is difficult to make long-distance relationships work, and a very high percentage of them fail, so unless you're convinced that this is the right person for you, try to find **someone closer and eliminate the continuous travel.**

Jenifer

My main concern with long-distance relationships is that you don't get to experience what everyday life is like with the other person. Every time you see each other, it's like a mini-vacation. **It is much easier to hold up a** certain persona when you don't see each other every day. **Often one person ends up relocating for or possibly even** marrying a person that they didn't get to know on the same level as a local relationship would have provided.

* * *

Do's and Don'ts

It may begin with eye contact, but the reality is that conversation gets you where you want to be.

Be Educated in Conversation

Jim

No profanity, period. Educated women aren't looking for a trailer-trash guy with a potty mouth. Enough said. It may begin with eye contact, but the reality is that conversation gets you where you want to be. The world is a big place, so before you go out to meet someone, take a little time to know what's going on in it—what are the hot topics locally, nationally, and internationally. Keep in mind that you don't want to talk about religion, sex, or politics until you get to know them a little better. When you do this, you become more interesting. When men are interesting, women want to learn more, which means spending time together. There is no substitute for face-to-face conversation, so keep **the phone chat fairly short until you meet again. Keep** in mind that although men are visual creatures, women are auditory, and the way for men to achieve their goal is **through the conversations you have and really listening to** what's said.

Jenifer

As I said earlier, being a good conversationalist will get
you a long way on a date. I agree, no profanity, being
well-spoken, and having the ability to talk about several
different topics will also get you a long way on a date. I'm
going to stick with what I said earlier in the communication
section. If you don't normally follow sports or stay up
on current events, don't study up on it real quick for
your date. It is important to be exactly who you are so
you can attract a person who likes you for exactly who
you are. Your relationship will not last long if you try to
be something you're not. If you choose to learn about
new things so that you can be more educated and more
interesting, choose topics that you are truly interested in
so that you are not misrepresenting yourself.

*   *   *

You will be a lot more interesting if you're out there living life instead of sitting home on your sofa watching TV.

Educated Versus Interesting

Jim

If you're reading this book, you then have the ability to become educated. There's a whole universe of options offering anything you would like to be educated in; however, I suggest for the purposes of dating that you **have an understanding of current events. This is pretty** easy to accomplish with a trip to the local bookstore and browsing through the magazines, listening to news on the radio or watching television. Whereas interesting, on the other hand, is different. Online dictionaries define *interesting* as **"holding the attention or arousing interest."** For men, if you're not sure what women find interesting in a man, then ask them, and once you begin to get a general consensus, consider those qualities and find a way to work them into your life. People enjoy the company of someone who's interesting. Mix educated with interesting, add confidence and a sense of humor, and your ability to attract a person will grow exponentially.

Jenifer

Being interesting has as much to do with your life experiences as with your education. You'll be a lot more interesting if you're out there living life instead of sitting home on your sofa watching TV. Learn a new hobby, take a trip, read a book, take up golf or maybe even learn to play a musical instrument or volunteer your time at a local charity. It doesn't really matter what you pursue, choose something you're passionate about and get involved. It would be best if you had a full life and then found someone to share it with as opposed to looking for someone else to fill up your life. Not only will you be more educated and interesting, but you'll also come across as less desperate and needy.

*   *   *

Hygiene

There are always some people that don't understand the need for proper hygiene. That means shower daily using **soap and shampoo. Wash your body thoroughly and** don't forget your ears. No woman wants to start working her tongue in your ear only to taste ear wax, so let the **Q-tips do their job. Keep your nails clean and trimmed** or manicured if possible. If you're not sure how they should look, then go get a manicure sometime and watch what the professionals do and follow suit. Shave when necessary, always brush your teeth, and consider using a tongue scraper (much of the bad breath people have is associated with their tongue) and some mouthwash. Be **clean-shaven and put on some lotion to keep your skin** smooth to the touch; however, if you are going to have facial hair, keep it highly groomed. A very high percentage of women do not prefer full beards, so if you have that big burly mountain-man beard and you think it looks great, **guess again; so trim or shave off that unruly barricade of** hair you call a beard, and don't forget those nose hairs reaching like tentacles for the outside world, and if you have hair in your ears, clean it up. Cologne/perfume can be nice, but never overdo it. *Never!* **Remember that less is better and quality matters. If you can only afford one** bottle of cologne/perfume, then buy quality, not quantity. Bad cologne/perfume can kill any prospects before you ever open your mouth. When choosing a fragrance, don't assume your nose knows; ask the person at the counter **since they should be the expert. This not only gives you** an informed opinion but also allows you to chat with a complete stranger, which should build your confidence in **conversations.**

*   *   *

You don't have to wear Armani or Prada to impress someone.

Dressing with a sense of style is important, and dressing appropriately for the occasion is equally important.

Dress Well

Jim

This is a common problem, so here you go, boys. You don't have to wear Armani or Ralph Lauren to impress a woman. If you don't have much of a sense of style, and many men don't, ask the opinion of a woman that's dressed nicely, preferably near your own age. Speaking of age, dress age appropriate; a woman doesn't want to see a forty-year-old dressed as a teenager. Just as you want to be seen with a woman that looks great, remember that she feels the same, so leave the NASCAR gear and the Dallas Cowboys jersey for the sports bars with the guys. If you're still not sure, then pick up a magazine like *GQ* **and** *Cosmopolitan Architectural Digest* and look how the people in the advertisements dress. Keep your clothes clean and wrinkle free, and dress with confidence.

Women typically look at three accessories when they meet a man—shoes, belt, and watch. Shoes should be nice, clean, not worn-out, and go well with what you have on. Belts should have a nice style and an appropriately nice buckle. You may want to have three or four belts for different situations, and since you only need a few, then spend the extra money. Watches are a different story. You can easily spend thousands on a single watch, but that's not necessary. You should have a minimum of two watches—a nice dress watch that you should plan on spending at least a few hundred dollars on and an everyday sports watch. Just remember the saying "The clothes make the man," so buy nice clothes over time until you have a complete wardrobe that can cover a variety of social situations.

Jenifer

You know what they say, "Nothing is sexier than a sharp-dressed man!" Dressing with a sense of style is important, and dressing appropriately for an occasion is equally important. We have talked about the importance of self-confidence throughout the book, and I can't stress how important your date outfit is for your self-confidence. Go out and purchase a couple of date outfits. It is important that you choose outfits that you feel excellent in. When you walk in that restaurant, you want to feel like a million bucks. Dressing in a specific date outfit will not only help you carry yourself with confidence (which is the most attractive thing a guy can wear), but it will also tell your date that you cared enough about meeting her to go the extra mile. Women like to feel that the date was important enough for you to take extra pride in your appearance; they also like to know that you are capable of dressing for the occasion. If you need help, you can always ask a salesperson close to your age to help, or if you can afford it, I would suggest hiring an image consultant to help you choose two or three date outfits.

*　*　*

If you immediately begin with talking about sex, you will turn them off, and the only sex you'll be seeing is with yourself.

Be Respectful

Jim

No swearing early on, period. After you know each other well, that can be a different story, but keep the risqué language to a minimum, and that includes sex talk. If you immediately begin with talking about sex, you will turn her off, and the only sex you'll be having is with yourself. Being respectful means being courteous, opening doors, helping her with her coat, thinking of her first, and making sure you're on time. She feels that her time is valuable, so treat it as such. Show that you have manners, especially table manners, because nobody wants to eat with a pig. Say please and thank you and really mean it. If you know you need to work on your manners, buy a book on etiquette **and practice it in every situation until it becomes** your second nature. If you work on having class, you will begin to stand above others, and as you master the art of class, people will begin to gravitate to you.

Jenifer

Most women are definitely attracted to men who behave **as gentlemen. We love to have the car door opened for** us, as well as allowing us to walk first through doors as we enter places together. Always let the woman order first when at a restaurant or ask her what she would like and order for her. Many women pay attention to the way her date treats the waitress. If you are rude to the waitress, it will indicate that you are not a very kind and considerate person. A sharp-dressed man with great manners, carrying himself with a sense of class and treating women with great respect, will rarely (if ever) get turned down for a second date. It will also help you get more first dates because women notice men like this in a roomful of people. I must add that most women (probably over 90 percent) are attracted to this type of behavior, but not all women. If you sense that she is not comfortable, it will **benefit you to simply ask her if she prefers that you open** her door for her. Obviously, if she doesn't prefer you to open her door, you may not want to order for her either.

*   *   *

Confident men don't need to be arrogant.

Arrogance is a sense of superiority; self-confidence is simply believing in yourself and your own abilities.

Be Confident, Not Arrogant

Jim

You must understand the difference between confidence and arrogance because you can bet that a woman knows the difference when she hears it. If you're not sure what the difference is, then get a dictionary. If you're not sure which one you are, then ask your friends if you are an a—hole sometimes. A yes means you need to lose the arrogance and begin learning confidence. Confident men don't need to be arrogant. Ask a woman what qualities she finds attractive in a man, and you will almost certainly hear confidence. Talking to women can be intimidating at first, but with time, you will become more self-assured. As you become accustomed to talking with women you don't know, you will find that your confidence grows. It can be difficult at first but must be done and is covered later in this book.

Jenifer

I have heard over and over that women want men who are self-confident, but not arrogant. Having self-confidence and a sense of self-worth is completely different from arrogance. Arrogance is a sense of superiority; self-confidence is simply believing in yourself and your own abilities, knowing what you bring to the table and being happy with that. It doesn't make you better than other people; it makes you happy with who you are.

*   *   *

Women like men who are playful and fun; we want to be with someone who makes us laugh and who doesn't take things too seriously.

Turn the Tables on Her

Jim

The game typically works that the man chases the woman and, if everything works out, catches her, and the relationship ensues. However, when you turn the tables on her, interesting things happen. When you're having a playful chat with her, you may say something funny like "You keep looking at me like you're hungry. You know I'm not a piece of meat." She may give you a strange look or maybe even laugh; if so, you can follow it up with "I know how you girls are, all hands, grabbing all over me, and I'm not that kind of guy." Follow that up by laughing at yourself. This works well, throws her off balance, and surprisingly enough, puts the message in her mind that she needs to chase you. You'll be amazed at the results, but don't overdo it or her demeanor may become somewhat prickly! She may also tell you that she doesn't pursue men, and in that case, you can say, "Then I guess I'll be your first." It may sound cocky, but if she has any sense of humor at all, the results will speak for themselves.

Jenifer

This playful type of exchange can be fun and will work well with the right type of personality. One word of caution, do not over do it because she will definitely become irritated! Women like men who are playful and fun; we want to be with someone who makes us laugh and who doesn't take **things too seriously. This behavior exhibits all those traits** but, if pushed too far, will become obnoxious. On the flip side, trying this out with a woman could give you a lot of insight into her personality as well. Is she playful enough to play back? How she responds could be very telling.

*   *   *

Having a positive attitude will improve all aspects of your life, including the dating and relationship aspect.

Have a Positive Outlook

Jim

Nobody wants to be around someone who's a downer, including someone you're dating. What they want to experience is someone with a positive outlook on life and everything that it entails. They want to be with someone that enjoys living life, not a spectator just watching it pass them by. You don't want to become involved with someone that's filled with negativity. You can't expect a happy, healthy person to be interested in you if when they're around you they feel as though they're slowly drowning. If you need help with this, the local bookstore has a whole section devoted to self-help.

Jenifer

We are naturally drawn to positive, upbeat people. If you want people to gravitate to you naturally, focus on the positive things in your life. You can find the good in just about everything if you look for it. You may have ten great things going on in your life and three not-so-great things. You have a choice—you can focus on the ten great things or you can focus on the three not-so-great things. Obviously, it would be better to focus on the ten great things, but it would be even better if you could find the positive things in the other three. Having a positive attitude will improve all aspects of your life, including the dating and relationship aspect. As I said earlier, if you are on a first date, make sure to keep it light and fun; do not talk about anything negative in your life, past or present. As the relationship develops, you will eventually share your past; try to focus on the positive things that evolved from your past experiences. Again, you can find the positive in even some of the worst situations or events.

*   *   *

When you're always available, then there's no challenge for her, and you become predictable and come across as clingy with no real social life.

Women want a man to be so taken with them that they can't wait to see them again.

Don't Always Be Available

Jim

Men tend to like it when women are at their beck and call, but when it comes to women, think again. When you are unavailable, a woman's first thought is "Who's he with?" When she wonders that, it stirs up her competitive nature and makes her want your time even more. This is a fine line; if you play this card too much, she will begin to lose interest and move on, but when done properly, it can be very effective. When you're always available, there's **no challenge for her; you become predictable and come across as clingy with no real social life.**

Jenifer

I'm sorry, Jim, but I don't agree with this one. I have heard this as a dating tip many times. It doesn't matter how many times I hear it, I just don't agree with it. Yes it's true that we want you to have a social life, but we also want you to invite us into it. Women want a man to be so taken with them that they can't wait to see them again. We want them to be thinking about ways to see us and places to take us. As a woman with a very full life, I am not looking **for someone to fill up my life but rather someone to share** my life with. I would want a man who also has a full life and is excited to bring me into it. I don't want to play games with people. If you're available, you're available. If you're not, you're not. I think it's extremely important to be exactly who you are and be honest about what you have to offer. If you have to play a game to catch a woman, **she probably isn't the right one for you. Keep a great social** life, and when you meet a wonderful woman, invite her into it. If you would enjoy her being there with you, invite her. Keep it simple, honest, and straightforward.

*   *   *

Don't Kiss and Tell

Jim

This is pretty simple, yet one of the most common **boneheaded mistakes men make. When you're fortunate** enough to engage physically with a woman at whatever level, she has decided that she can trust you. When you blab about it and she finds out, she naturally feels betrayed and upset, so don't be surprised if you never get another **chance to get close to her. You can apologize until you're** blue in the face, but your big mouth has already wrecked what could have been, so keep your yap shut and deserve the trust she placed in you. As for women, most men **could really care less if you decide to share the steamy** details with your friends, but it's still better to keep things just between the two of you rather than find out that you crossed a line with him.

Jenifer

What more is there to say? Except that as adults, it's a little scary that we even have to cover this.

*   *   *

Your success or failure in attracting people may very well depend on your ability to carry intelligent conversation.

Those who are great conversationalist rarely get turned down for a second date.

Navigating the Conversation Minefield

Jim

I touched on this before, and this is one of the most important building blocks for men to work on. I don't know if women understand just how difficult it can be for a man to strike up a conversation with a woman they find attractive. Your success or failure in attracting women may very well depend on your ability to carry intelligent conversation. **It begins by simply talking to strangers and** is easier than you may think. Start with your server at the restaurant or the checker at the grocery store, etc. Most people really want to talk about themselves and are simply waiting for the opportunity. As we know, women are eager to chat it up, but you must have good questions. I said good questions, not "How about that weather?" Go deeper with something like "Did you grow up in this area?" When they tell you where they grew up, follow up with "What is it like there this time of year?" and "Have you lived here long?" These are all simple questions, and eventually, you will build a cache of questions that have gotten the best responses. As your confidence grows, you will find that your questions seem to be more powerful, and the responses more interesting. As you force yourself to do this daily, you'll notice that it becomes easier to meet women that you're interested in. Keep practicing and remember to be respectful. Don't worry if you get shot down because there are more than eighty-nine million single Americans out there, and just as you may not be interested in every woman, they may not be into you, so don't take it personally and just move on.

Jenifer

As I said earlier, to be great at dating, you must be a great conversationalist. I have found that those who are great conversationalist rarely get turned down for the second date. And of course, the second date is very important. If you never get past the first date, there is no chance of a relationship evolving. Practice being a good conversationalist and use every opportunity you have to develop this skill. If you find yourself on a bad date, don't waste it; use it as an opportunity to hone your communications skills. If you get invited to someone's house for dinner or to a party, use these events as the perfect place to polish being interested and interesting. These are the two keys to being a great conversationalist. You must present yourself as an interesting person, and you must be genuinely interested in learning about the other person. Always ask open-ended questions, and if asked a question, make sure to elaborate on the answer and then ask a question in return. When you communicate, remember to use a good eye contact. I know it's hard when you're nervous, but it makes a huge difference because without eye contact, you will not come across as engaging or sincere. I couldn't agree with Jim more—practice, practice, and then practice some more. Some people are more outgoing than others, but almost everyone can better prepare in this area. You may be the type of person that can walk up and talk to anyone, but it's usually different when you come across a person you're interested in. You need to be talking about the right things, be positive, and equally as interested in learning about them as you are talking about yourself.

*   *   *

By laughing at yourself, people see the lighter side of your personality, and it draws them in.

Sense of Humor

Jim

This is a must and usually starts with the ability to laugh at yourself. By laughing at yourself, people see the lighter side of your personality, and it draws them in. Everyone loves to laugh, and if you look around, you'll notice that many average men with a good sense of humor are with *hot* women; and when asked, the woman invariably says, "He made me laugh." This doesn't mean be a clown, and it's important to understand when humor is appropriate, but certainly, don't underestimate the power of humor.

Jenifer

Humor is a must and certainly one of the top five personality characteristics I get asked for when my clients are setting criteria for the types of people they would like to meet. A nice woman told me during an interview that she was looking for a man that had the ability to create fun. When I questioned her further, she said that when most people don't have anything to do, they sit around and complain about being bored. She wanted to meet a man with a good sense of humor, but to take it one step further, she wanted someone that could create fun. When she said it, it sounded so simple and obvious, but I had never thought of it that way. Have a sense of humor, don't take yourself or life to seriously, be fun loving, and learn how to create fun. Once you accomplish this, I can assure you, women will be drawn to you.

*   *   *

Women lose interest in the guy that's too nice because they come across as almost spineless and weak.

As long as you don't confuse being nice with being a pushover, I say there is no such thing as being too nice.

Don't Be Too Nice

Jim

Women over thirty usually have had enough experiences with the bad boy and are ready for the nice guy; however there is a tipping point when a guy can be too nice. Women lose interest in the guy that's too nice because they come across as almost spineless and weak. Don't be that guy; be nice but think for yourself too. Make a stand from time to time for what you want, and you'll find that she appreciates you all the more.

Jenifer

I would agree that as women become older, *nice* becomes a lot more important. The problem is that everyone has a different definition of *nice*. Nice does not make you spineless, and it certainly doesn't mean always giving the other person their way. When people ask me for a nice person, I always ask them what *nice* means to them. It's amazing the variety of answers I get, but here are a few of the most popular:

- Thoughtful

- Genuinely caring of others

- Loving

- Generous with the time and attention they give to their family, friends, and the community in which they live

I have never had anyone ask me for a bad boy, and I have had thousands ask me for a truly nice, kindhearted person. As long as you don't confuse being nice with being a pushover, I say there is no such thing as being too nice.

*   *   *

There's really not much you can do but apologize and feel like a moron.

Forgetting Their Name

Jim

This happens to everyone at one time or another and is always embarrassing, not just for you but for them also. Before you meet or go on your date, do whatever is necessary to memorize their name even if you have to write it somewhere inconspicuous so you can glance at it when necessary. If it still happens to you, it's usually going to be when you're expected to introduce them to someone, so all you can do is apologize, letting them know that you're not sure what happed and that you're extremely embarrassed and ask for their forgiveness. There's really not much you can do but apologize and feel like a moron.

Jenifer

If you forget her name, you should just pack up, go home, and move on. Just kidding. Jim is right; if it happens, there's not much else you can do other than apologize profusely. She may or may not be offended by it, and you'll just have to accept whatever comes of it.

* * *

Player Versus Womanizer

The player is someone that's actively in the game, understands how women like to be treated, gives them the proper respect, and is courteous even during a breakup. A womanizer, however, is a jerk and a self-absorbed jackass that will do anything to get what he wants. This type of predator gives most men a bad name and leaves women thinking that all men are jerks. He thrives on destroying self-esteem, creating problems where none existed, controlling her every move, and generally making life miserable. Men like this rarely have female friends and will never enjoy the benefits that female friends can offer. This guy thinks he's cool and is constantly bragging about his exploits to anyone that'll listen. If you're this guy, then you're a loser and should rethink your strategy for the future. If you're too stupid to heed this warning, then prepare to grow old alone because although many young women are drawn to the jerk, they mature and learn to avoid him, seeking instead someone that will treat them properly.

*   *   *

If you don't give them any space, you may come across as a very clingy person or a person without a life.

Give Them Space

Jim

When you're just beginning to date someone that you really like, the sparks are flying, you think about each other all the time, it feels like you can't get enough of each other, and it almost feels like a drug. Take a short step back and remember that you still need balance in your life as does this new person you desire. Give them some space; suggest that they spend time with their friends and family, and you should do the same. If what you have is real, then it will still be there after the time spent with friends and family. You may actually find that it will make for a much healthier relationship should the two of you decide to enter into one.

Jenifer

Space and pacing yourself are both important. If you don't give them any space, you may come across as a very clingy person or a person without a life. When you meet someone that you really like, it can be exactly like a drug, and you can hardly stay away from them. The problem with not pacing yourself is that it will be really hard to maintain this level of time commitment and drug like high. When it starts to take on some normalcy, it will create disappointment, and both of you will be wondering why the relationship has changed and start to question it. When it gets to the normal level, you may feel like it fizzled out because it was out of proportion in the first place. I must give you one warning. My advice is not to go slow like a snail. If you meet someone you like, call her within twenty-four to forty-eight hours, make plans to see her regularly, move the relationship forward. People want to feel like you are excited about them. You need to find balance here. Balance is the key to most things, and this is no exception.

*   *   *

Recognize when you're being phony; stop the behavior and be your true self.

Being Phony

Jim

There is a difference between being phony and being a liar. Phony people fake interest in subjects that they know interests a person just to achieve their short-range goals. Sometimes they actually believe that they could be interested in the same things just to justify in their minds the connection with the person they desire. Recognize when you're being phony; stop the behavior and be your true self. You may just find that they're still interested in you. If you continue to be phony, you may end up standing in the rain without an umbrella.

There is more than one type of being phony and one that men particularly hate is a tease. The phrase *she's a tease* originated with some guy out there that was frustrated, and nobody likes to be teased. What it really means is that flirts with a man send him signals that she is interested in him and keep him dangling at the end of her line but never reels him in for anything more intimate. There is a term for women that tease men to get attention; they are known as attention whores. These women are usually attractive yet very insecure and seem eternally starved for attention. Avoid these women as they will rarely give you what you want and love nothing more than stringing you along and wasting your time and money. Men, on the other hand, don't tease women with enticement of actually being more interested than they are because if they're interested at all, you'll know by their actions.

Jenifer

No point in being phony. Complete waste of everyone's time. You need to find someone who wants to be with you just the way you are. You may become interested in some of the things they like, and they may become interested in some of the things you like. That is simply part of exploring a relationship. Half the fun of meeting someone new is being introduced to people and things that weren't already a part of your life. You don't need to pretend that you are interested in the same things; you just need to be open to trying new things and finding common interests.

*   *   *

Remember that you're all friends and should be playing wingman for each other, working as a team so that all of you can obtain what you're seeking.

Competing against Friends

Jim

This is not only stupid but can be unnecessarily detrimental to your friendship. When you're with a group of your friends, decide who gets to take the first shot when **more than one of you is interested in the same person. There are far too many single people for you to compete** with your friends. That being said, if the first person gets shot down, then the door should still be open for whoever **is next. Remember that you're all friends and should be** playing wingman for each other, working as a team so that all of you can obtain what you're seeking.

Jenifer

No clue. Women don't do this. ☺

* * *

If you lie about the little things how do you expect someone to trust you when it really matters.

It is important that you are honest about all things and build trust right from the beginning.

Liars

Jim

This is a big one. If you are a compulsive liar, then get professional help. If you lie about little things, how do you expect someone to trust you when it really matters? When you're interested in someone that lies to you, call them on it every time and keep a mental note. If they can't seem to help it, then dump them. Life is too short to wonder if they're being honest, and it's really not worth the effort in the long run. If they're not an honest person, then what could you ever really have with them other than some steamy sex? And if that's the case, do it and move on. Don't fall into their web of deceit as it can only take you places you don't want to go.

Jenifer

Earlier I said sense of humor was in the top five personality characteristics people ask me for when setting criteria for the people they would like to meet. Well, honesty is also in the top five and probably in the top three. Even a small lie in the beginning of a relationship has the potential to completely change the path of that relationship. It is important that you are honest about all things and build trust right from the beginning. As far as the steamy sex comment goes, I wouldn't even want to have steamy sex with a liar because they might be lying about having herpes! Don't lie about the small stuff, the big stuff, or anything in between, and run from them if you catch them lying—run as fast as you can!

*   *   *

Be secure enough in who you are and what you project and leave the name-dropping to the doorknobs that think it makes them cool.

If you have to brag about the people you know in high places, it indicates that you lack self-confidence and can come across as obnoxious.

Name-droppers

Jim

I think we have all experienced the person that wants you **to think they're somebody and goes about it by dropping** famous names. My opinion is that famous people are just people, and though they have achieved a level of fame, they are no better or worse than anyone else. So be secure enough in who you are and what you project and leave the name-dropping to the doorknobs who think it makes them cool. Trust me when I say that most people are turned off by name-droppers, so don't do it.

Jenifer

I've had a few name-dropping clients over the years, and I must say people do not find it attractive. It's okay to bring names up in general conversation and to talk about some of the people you know. However, do not force the conversation to continue in this direction and do not bring up an important name every time they make a comment about something. Above all, do not keep saying things like "I'm sure you know . . ." and "Have you ever met . . ." This will make your date feel inadequate and will be a major turn off. Quiet self-confidence is attractive; if you brag about the people you know in high places, it indicates that you lack self-confidence and can come across as obnoxious.

*   *   *

When you interrupt them, it is not only rude, but it also tells them that what you have to say is more important than what they were saying and that while they were talking you weren't really listening, but thinking about what you wanted to say.

Interrupters

Jim

Conversation goes like this. They talk, then when there is an opening, you talk and so forth. When you interrupt them, it is not only rude, but it also tells them that what you have to say is more important then what they were saying and that while they were talking you weren't really listening, but thinking about what you wanted to say. So don't interrupt, and if they constantly interrupt you, then call them on it and ask them to stop. If they can't stop, then it's likely that they really don't care what you have to say anyway. Time to give them the ham sandwich and the road map—they're out of here!

Jenifer

I think we've all been guilty of interrupting at one point or another. Question is, do you make a regular habit of it? If so, you really need to work on your conversation skills. I've been talking all through the book about how being a good conversationalist will make you a good dater. Constantly interrupting during a conversation is definitely not being a good conversationalist. It is so important to be interested in what the other person has to say. How in the world will you know if you want to plan another date with this person if you never let them talk or were not listening when they were talking? I know you have a lot to say, and I'm sure you're thinking that you need to tell this person all the great things about yourself so they will want to go out with you again. *Wrong!* They will want to go out with you again if you seemed truly interested in them and if they enjoyed the time spent with you. Neither of these things will happen if you are constantly interrupting. Yes, you need to share information about yourself, but then be quiet and let them share too.

*   *   *

Talking about your ex is a negative subject, and there's a chance that talking about it could bring up emotions of anger, disappointment, resentment, sadness, etc.

Ex This, Ex That

Jim

They don't want to hear about your ex's or past dates just as you probably don't want to hear about theirs. If they ask, then you can touch on it lightly but don't dwell on it. In conversations, they may bring up their ex's or past dates, but try to steer it in a different direction. The one gem you may get from listening to them talk about their past relationships is that they will undoubtedly tell you about some traits or characteristics that they despise, so remember those tidbits, and if possible, use them to your advantage.

Jenifer

This is the number one biggest mistake made on a first date and in relationships in general. From your initial meeting on, avoid talking about your ex. The first date is a time for the two of you to find out what you have in common, your similar goals and desires, etc. If you spend your time talking about your ex or your ugly divorce, several things will happen. Have you ever heard the saying about never getting a second chance to make a first impression? Of course you have. Talking about your ex is a negative subject, and there's a chance that talking about it could bring up emotions of anger, disappointment, resentment, sadness, etc. Before you know it, they are sharing with you their latest breakup as well, and the whole conversation has become negative and very heavy. This is your first impression, so it is important to keep the conversation light, happy, positive, and fun. The other problem with talking about your ex or all your latest dates is that you are not spending your time getting to know each other. This date is about the two of you—today.

It is not about the past or even about what happened yesterday or on last week's date; it is about this date right now, so make the most of it. If you're long past your first date and in a relationship, it's still imperative that you don't dwell on your ex's. Get over it and move on. Learn from whatever experience you had with that person and use it to make your future better. None of us want to hear **people talk about those in their past all the time. It leads** us to believe two things: One is that you're not over that relationship completely (if you were, you wouldn't be bringing it up all the time); and two, that we are constantly being compared to the other person. We want to know that we are unique and that you appreciate that about us. Even if you're saying that we are better than the other person, the fact that you brought her up means you're **thinking about her.**

When you begin having conversations about religion and politics, always be respectful of their personal opinion, whether you agree with it or not.

Left Wing, Right Wing

Jim

Most people have an opinion when it comes to politics; however, it may be a good idea for you to keep your political views to yourself. If your date brings it up and you're like-minded, then you may choose to share your thoughts. More than one person has blurted out their political views only to find their date has opposing ideas, which can be a date crusher. It's certainly not worth arguing over, so keep it to yourself, and if your date brings it up, bite your tongue.

Jenifer

People often say that you should never talk about politics or religion on the first date. I have mixed feelings about this. Early in the book, we talked about deciding what you really want and determining what your deal breakers are. If politics and religion are on your deal breaker list, you're going to need to bring it up early in the relationship to determine if this is a person you feel has views and beliefs that you can live with. Some people feel that each person is entitled to their own views and beliefs, and it doesn't bother them if they differ from their own. Others feel that they really want to be with someone who shares the same beliefs and views. Which one are you? It would benefit you to determine this and proceed with dating accordingly. If it doesn't matter that much to you, I agree that you should leave it out of the conversation. It could make the other person feel uncomfortable, or they may misread your intention and feel that it is important to you and that's why you brought it up. If you determine that it's very important to you, I would still recommend that you wait and bring it up on the second or third date, again making every effort to keep the first interactions light and fun. When you begin having conversations about religion and politics, always be respectful of their personal opinion, whether you agree with it or not.

*   *   *

If you get sloppy drunk and make a fool of yourself on your date, then you probably won't get another one.

Your date doesn't want to show up to find that you are already drinking; it can send off red flags.

Alcohol

Jim

Going out for drinks can help break the ice and make the conversation lively, but don't overdo it. If you're driving, know your limit and the law. It's better to take a cab home if in doubt or, better yet, take a cab all evening. If you prefer to take a cab, you still need to monitor your alcohol intake. If you get sloppy drunk and make a fool of yourself on your date, then you probably won't get another one. If your date is the one that overdoes it, then do what you can to keep them out of trouble and get them home safely. This means getting them home safely, not going back to their place and taking advantage of them. Men, be a gentleman, and she will remember you if you force yourself on her, and expect to go to jail and rightfully so. Some people should just not drink because they get weird. If they're one of those, get them to the front door but don't go in because you don't want them accusing you of something that never happened.

Jenifer

It's Just Lunch started as a personalized dating service that sent people out on lunch dates. The concept was that lunch was low-key and a lot less pressure than dinner. Over the years, we found that many professionals could not meet for lunch as they did not have traditional schedules. Since we cater to busy professionals, we decided to add drinks after work as one of the options for the date. I learned very quickly that people preferred drinks after work to lunch. About 75 percent of the dates I coordinate in my offices are for drinks. I became curious and started asking questions about why so many clients were choosing drinks (even the clients that don't drink alcohol) instead of lunch. The first date is all about getting to know each other; this means a lot of talking is probably going to happen. Most people find it awkward to talk while they eat, worried about whether or not something is stuck in their teeth or if they are talking with their mouth full, etc. The women told me they felt a lot more comfortable meeting for a glass of wine or a cocktail. If you don't drink alcohol, you could always order a virgin drink, ice tea, or coffee. The men told me that they prefer a drink after work because if it was going well, they could invite the lady to join them for dinner and end up spending more time with her, moving it into a more romantic setting. In other words, the drinks were the introduction to see if a connection appeared, and then the dinner was the date. Men and women had different reasons for preferring drinks to lunch, but regardless, it's the most popular and the least stressful. Now that we know so many people prefer drinks, you can see why the things Jim was addressing are so important. Too much alcohol will be a killer on the first date. Don't show up early so you can have a drink before your date arrives. Believe it or not, a lot of people do this because they think they will be more relaxed. Your date doesn't want to show up to find that you are already drinking; it can send off red flags. Your date also wants to have intelligent conversation with you throughout the evening, so pacing yourself is important. Pay special attention to everything Jim said because boy, was he right.

*   *   *

Nothing is worse than someone on the other end of the phone slurring their words and thinking they're sexy.

Drunk Dialing

Jim

Be very careful with this. Usually, people drunk dial **because they're hoping for sex. If it's simply a booty call** and you're up for it, then it may be okay, but if you're still just getting to know them you may turn them off completely. You can call the following day and apologize, but some people take offense, especially knowing that the person just wanted one thing. So control yourself and don't do it, but should you do it anyway, don't be surprised if you get unwanted results.

Jenifer

Nothing is worse than someone on the other end of the phone slurring their words and thinking they're sexy. Fortunately, most people dial their ex when drunk, and since this relationship is already over, you can't do much damage, except maybe the bruised ego the next day because you broke down and called. If you happen to call someone you are in a new relationship with, it probably won't be good. Moderation is the key to everything in life.

I say, drink with moderation, and you won't have to worry about this.

*   *   *

You can go get help or you can go to jail;
there is not much in between.

Stalking

Jim

I hate this subject and shouldn't have to cover it, but people are out there that don't understand just how crazy stalking really is. If they aren't interested in you, let them be and move on. If you are fixated on them, then get **some professional help for the disorder. You can go get** help or you can go to jail; there is not much in between. If you're being stalked, then ask them to stop and let them know that you will be contacting the authorities about the problem. Be sure to document every situation in which you **encountered the stalker and seek legal advice. Should you** have to get a restraining order, then the judge will need **the documentation.**

Jenifer

Jim nailed it again, and I don't have much to add. The **only thing I might say is that sometimes one person** **thinks they are being stalked and the other person has** no idea why they feel this way. The only thing I can think **is that not everyone has the same definition of stalking.** Here are some general guidelines: Do not show up at **someone's house unless you are invited. If you call three** times and don't get a return phone call, do not call again!

If they don't tell you where they live, don't use modern technology to determine their address. Nothing will freak someone out more than you finding out where they live without them telling you. The same goes for where they work. If they do not offer this information, do not go looking for it. If someone is not responding to you positively by returning phones calls, etc., move on!

*   *   *

If you're desperate, you will agree to anything, and they'll spot it as weakness and either manipulate you or dump you. Either way—poof—they're gone.

Don't be afraid to let a person know that you're very attracted to them and that you want to see them again tomorrow or this weekend; just make sure you do it in a way that displays self-confidence, not clinginess.

Don't Be Desperate

Jim

Many men are somewhat smitten by a woman after a first date and can become cling-ons (clingy), which is a major turn off for the second date. Keep your confidence, don't be arrogant, but believe to a degree that they're lucky to be with you. Hopefully, this will remove a little of your insecurity. By the time this date has arrived, you should already have spoken on the phone and discussed what type of restaurant you want, but watch it if you go to the movies. Men should know that women may test you and ask if you can go to a chick flick instead of the movie you had agreed on. Don't let them do it and just tell her that they should see that movie with their friends, not you. If you're desperate, you will agree to anything, and they'll spot that as weakness and either manipulate you or dump you. Either way—poof—she's gone.

Jenifer

Jim, Jim, Jim, I could not disagree with you more. I agree that cling-ons are a major turn off, but that is about the only thing I agree with here. I should point out that knowing what you like when you see it and making it **clear is actually a turn on. Don't be afraid to let a person** know that you're very attracted to them and that you want to see them again; just make sure you do it in a way that displays self-confidence not clinginess. People want to feel like they took your breath away the minute they walked in the door. So don't be a cling-on, but have **enough self-confidence to say that you enjoyed yourself** so much you'd like to do it again real soon. Now as for the chick flick, as women, we go to plenty of "shoot 'em up" movies with you! Guys, yes, it's a test, and the test is "Will it always be all about you" as well as "Are you in touch with your feminine side enough to not only see a chick flick but to also actually enjoy it?" It's an important test, and I would suggest that you try to pass it. However, in this case, since you've already agreed on the movie, I would stick to **the agreement and promise to take her to the chick flick** next week. This shows that you are not a pushover, and it doesn't always have to be about you and what you like.

*   *   *

Recognition

When you don't recognize the signs, in the woman's mind, you become more like a stalker than a simple dumbass that doesn't get it.

Being persistent is a good thing to a certain degree, but at the end of the day, you want to be with someone who wants to be with you.

Recognize When They Aren't into You

Jim

This part is more of a public service for women than for you men. When you don't recognize the signs, in the woman's mind, you become more like a stalker than a simple dumbass that doesn't get it. Not answering the phone when you call and never returning your calls is a pretty strong signal that you don't do it for her. If you're sitting at a table together and she's inspecting every guy that walks by, guess what, she's really not into you. If you ask her out and she continually makes excuses about why she can't go, then stop asking and move on. She's not the only fish in the sea, so you shouldn't treat her as such. Just because you want her doesn't mean that she is like-minded, so do yourself and her a favor and just leave her alone. If she chats with you on the phone but never accepts your date invitations, then she is probably just being nice, so be nice also and stop asking her out.

Jenifer

If a woman is really interested in a man, she will make time for him. If she is always telling you she is too busy to get together, then one of two things is true: She is really not that into you, or she is not ready to make time for a relationship in her life. In either case, you need to move on. Truth is, if someone really likes you, they'll make time to see you. **Being persistent is a good thing to a certain degree,** but at the end of the day, you want to be with someone who wants to be with you. Trying to force it never works. Even if she gives in and goes out with you because you were relentless, the reality is, she's not really **that into you.**

*   *   *

You're Only Too Old When She Thinks You Are

Many men are attracted to younger women but are unsure of how much younger is too young. There is no defining line, and it's different from woman to woman, so you need to establish what age-group she's looking for. Just as many men seek younger women, older women may do the same, so don't be disappointed if a woman close to your age is uninterested in you. Finding out what age range a woman prefers may be difficult to ask when meeting in person for the first time, but the signs of a woman being interested in you are the same for all age ranges. The only real difference is that older women may be more direct. The only way to be sure is to go for it, and don't be disappointed if she rejects you.

*   *   *

If you run into someone who gave you a wrong number, don't confront them as this will only be embarrassing for both of you.

Wrong Numbers

Jim

So, guys, you met this woman, asked for her number, and she actually gave it to you without hesitation, then you **called her only to find out that there's no such number or that the person on the other end informs you that** you have the wrong number. Accept the fact that the woman wasn't interested in you and didn't want to create any unwanted tension, so she simply did what she was comfortable with and slipped you the wrong number. **Don't take it personally; remind yourself that there are** plenty of women out there and that at least she didn't waste your time by leading you on. If you see her again, ignore her. Never confront her as you will only come across as a creep with issues that she would never ever go out with.

Jenifer

I actually think this is pretty rare. Normally, women will say they are in a relationship as a polite way to get out of giving you the number without hurting your feelings. Some women are not comfortable giving their phone number to a stranger, and so they may ask for your number instead.

This is often legitimate, so don't be put off if it happens. I agree that if you run into someone who gave you a wrong number, don't confront them as this will only be embarrassing for both of you.

*   *   *

Only you can decide what level of intelligence you prefer in a person or more importantly what level you're willing to accept.

Being a good intellectual match is an important part of having a relationship that will last.

Not the Brightest Bulb

Jim

It is impolite to refer to someone as dumb, but the truth is that some people are just plain "dumb as a mud fence." Only you can decide what level of intelligence you prefer in a person or more importantly what level you're willing to accept. Should you choose this type of person, keep in mind that you may find the relationship taxing and frustrating at times. The benefit is that most of these people are aware of their limited brain power and don't mind you making most of the important decisions. It's really this simple—are they really what you want? However you answer, that should be the determining factor in your decision.

Jenifer

When you are determining your preferences and deal
breakers, you'll have to decide where this falls on the list.
I can say that most people are attracted to intelligence. It
doesn't have to be formal education, but a certain level of
intelligence, worldliness, and street smarts are attractive
traits. Being a good intellectual match is an important
part of having a relationship that will last. You should
determine what a good intellectual match for you would
be before you get started in your search. Some people are
more attracted to people physically, and others are more
attracted to people mentally. You'll have to decide what
level of importance you want to put on intelligence and
being a good intellectual match. I suggest you give it some
serious thought.

*   *   *

There are men (usually older) that don't mind if a woman is a gold digger because they are willing to trade their money to have a hot woman on their arm to impress their friends.

A gold digger is a person that only dates wealthy men because they have money, not because they are truly in love with them.

Recognizing Gold Diggers

Jim

The term *gold digger* commonly refers to women, so I am writing that way. It's common for women to enjoy nice things. The question is, how did they obtain them? And if you become involved, will they expect you to provide them? The key is in finding out how they came about having these expensive trinkets. First you must recognize the difference of what is nice and what is average. Magazines are full of designers, and therein you have the opportunity to see what the logos look like. If you find that she is covered and accessorized with famous designers, **it is very possible that someone else purchased them for**

her. However, many women purchase these things with their own money, so approach the subject carefully and assume that she purchased them herself until you find otherwise. There are men (usually older) that don't mind if a woman is a gold digger because they're willing to trade their money to have a hot woman on their arm to impress their friends. This typically doesn't last. When the man gets older and the woman already has all the trinkets she wants, then she'll trade him in for a younger man. Don't waste your time with gold diggers as it can be a money pit with no guarantees of anything more. Gold diggers are really not much more than prostitutes that trade their bodies for expensive baubles.

Jenifer

First let's clarify what a gold digger is. A gold digger is a person that only dates wealthy men because they have money, not because they are truly in love with them. If a woman happens to fall in love with a wealthy man and he chooses to buy her nice things, it doesn't make her a gold digger. If you are a man of means, I would suggest that when you find someone you are interested in dating, you lay low. No need to expose the fact that you are wealthy right from the beginning. In other words, leave the Rolex, expensive suit, and fancy car at home. No need to talk about the fact that you have a second vacation house in a tropical location either. Just keep that information to yourself for a while and see if she accepts a second, third, and fourth date with you. You'll be glad later that you handled it this way. If you start dating, you'll always know that she likes you for who you are and chose to spend time with you before finding out that you were wealthy.

*   *   *

The only time they really care about you is if you have or can do something they want.

Self-Centered People

Jim

Everyone has experienced someone that's self-centered. It's all about them and always will be. The only time they really care about you is if you have or can do something they want. Most of them are chronically late as they believe that nobody's time is as valuable as their own. They insist on having everything exactly as they want it with no regard to what others may want. Simply put, they can't get enough of themselves. Recognize their behavior early on and avoid wasting your time as they're unlikely to change.

Jenifer

Why would anyone want to spend a significant amount of time with someone who only thinks about themselves? If you have ended up with this type of person several times in your past, you may want to give some serious thought why you are attracted to self-centered people. There is a reason, and you won't be able to change it until you figure out what the draw is for you. Once the draw is determined, you'll be more aware of it, and hopefully, you can change the pattern.

No matter how great your life is, they will want to mess it up with a drama that's unnecessary and overblown.

If they can't find real drama, they create it. They're only comfortable in crisis mode, and they don't even realize it.

Drama Queens

Jim

This is one of the most dreaded of women, but there are also many men that act this way. No matter how great your life is, they will want to mess it up with a drama that's unnecessary and overblown. They will constantly turn **nothing into something and act as though everything is life** or death, and if you're not on board with it, they'll make that into drama too. There is really no way to win with this type of person unless you're a drama queen too. Unless you're into drama, avoid this type of person.

Jenifer

Unless you enjoy drama, *run* and run fast. This type of person rarely changes. They invite drama into their lives, and then they feed off it. If they can't find real drama, they create it. They're only comfortable in crisis mode, and they don't even realize it.

*   *   *

You'll never be able to supply them with all the energy they need, so when you recognize one of these energy vampires, steer clear and find someone that gives as much energy as they take.

Energy Stealers

Jim

There are some people that will steal your energy and probably won't even realize that they're doing it. You'll notice that each time you're around them, you feel drained, and if you spend too much time with them, you find yourself exhausted. **You'll never be able to supply them with all the energy they need, so when you recognize one of these energy vampires, steer clear and find someone that gives as much energy as they take.**

Jenifer

When you are setting your original preferences and deal breakers list, you should consider energy levels. It is important to choose someone who is close to the same energy level as you. As far as energy stealers go, this usually refers to a person who is not very upbeat. You have to use all your energy to keep the relationship upbeat as they do not do it naturally. This has happened to me before, and it took me a long time to figure out what was going on. I knew he was a great guy and everything I was looking for in a lot of ways, but at the same time, I knew something was wrong and couldn't put my finger on it. It wasn't until years later when I was looking back that I finally figured out he was an energy stealer. They make you feel like the lifeblood is being sucked out of you. This is something most people aren't thinking about when searching for a potential mate, yet it is very important. Keep it in the back of your mind so you'll recognize it if it ever happens to you.

*   *   *

They constantly make excuses as to why they can't meet with you and continue to insist on how much they want to get together, but it just doesn't materialize.

Elusive People

Jim

There are many reasons for people to be elusive. The most common is that they just aren't that into you and are keeping you around until they find someone that they really are into. It could be that they're already seeing someone or maybe even married. These people will continue to string you along and sound interested, but when the time comes to getting together, they find reasons for it not to happen. They constantly make excuses as to why they can't meet with you and continue to insist on how much they want to get together, but it just doesn't materialize. Stop wasting your time and find someone else. You can bet that if they were really into you, they would make time for you.

Jenifer

My personal and professional opinion on this is that they're elusive because they don't really want to be in a relationship with you; they are trying to be nice and don't want to hurt your feelings. A person truly interested in having a relationship with you will not be acting elusive.

*   *   *

The sad thing is that even when you give them the control they want, they will become unhappy or even angry, thinking that they have to make all the decisions and do everything.

If she agrees to plans for the both of you without asking you first, address it immediately.

Controlling People

Jim

The struggle for power and control usually begins innocently enough. **If you don't recognize the signs and stand up for yourself early on, you will eventually become a doormat and have a miserable existence. It** begins simply enough by them changing plans without **your consent and expecting you to go along because** they're used to getting their way. It moves swiftly into them, asking you to spend time with them instead of doing things with your friends or family. Then they begin insisting that you check with them before you **make plans just in case they have scheduled you to do** something else. Before you know, it you're asking them **for permission to do anything. This is the most slippery** of slopes, and once you begin to slide, there is usually no way back until you break the control by ending the relationship. The sad thing is that even when you give them the control they want, they become unhappy or even angry, thinking that they have to make all the decisions and do everything. Eventually, they'll feel that you're not their equal and start wishing they had a partner that would make half of the decisions. Either way, you lose. So address this problem early and understand that it's their own insecurities that causing issue. It's fine to give in to their requests from time to time, but make sure you stand your ground and follow through with what you were planning to do with your friends or family and understand that when you come home, they may be upset or pout, but don't feel bad and remind them that you are not asking for anything more than you are willing to give. Don't ever ask their permission to do something. Lay down some rules concerning decision making and doing things together. This doesn't mean don't communicate; it just means there are times you need to stand your ground and be equal in the relationship. They will respect you for it more in the long run.

Jenifer

There is a difference between a strong person, self-confident person, and a controlling person. When you decide what you really want in a person, take some time to think about this one. Some people prefer for the other person to make all the decisions, be in charge of the social calendar, etc. Others will be driven crazy by this type of situation. I recommend having an agreement that you check with each other before committing to any plans for the other person. In other words, if your friend calls and asks the two of you to come to dinner on Friday night, your answer should be, "Let me run it by (insert name here) and I'll call you back to confirm." If you're both following the same guidelines, it is hard for one person to get too much control. If she agrees to plans for the both of you without asking you first, address it immediately. It will be harder to address it later if you've always been accepting of it. She will not understand why it needs to change.

*   *   *

This is really just a slow attack on you, and over time, you might not even notice it's happening, but it has deep and lasting effects.

It's hard to undo the damage of verbal abuse, so be on the lookout for the signs early in the relationship.

Abusive People

Jim

It starts with something like, "You dummy," and elevates to "Don't be stupid," leading to more hurtful and consistently harsh language. The person often doesn't know that they're doing it, and over time, it will wear down your self-esteem, eventually leading to depression. This is really just a slow attack on you, and you might not even notice it's happening, but it has deep and lasting effects. If your friends or family say things like, "I can't believe you let them talk to you that way." Listen closely to the words your significant other actually uses when speaking to you. When your ears are opened again, you will almost become **hypersensitive to the language that's used and see it for the ugliness that it is. If this has been happening and you** want to save the relationship, then counseling for the both of you is a must. If they refuse to go, it's because they're afraid of being exposed, and if you can't convince them of the importance of getting help, then you need to end the relationship. This won't get better without help. You should also be conscious of what words are coming out of your own mouth and make sure that you're not the one that's verbally abusive.

Jenifer

I have dated a couple of people who had come out of a verbally abusive relationship. What Jim said is exactly true. These people had no self-worth. One of the people **had been teased so much about their appearance that** they were actually embarrassed of the way they looked even though they were very attractive. It's hard to undo the damage of verbal abuse, so be on the lookout for the signs early in the relationship. If you see any signs, **move on quickly. Don't bother getting in a relationship** with someone and then try to fix them. They need to fix themselves before they get in a relationship with anyone.

*   *   *

When They Might Be Cheating

Jim

This should only apply if you both are in agreement about dating each other exclusively. You need to know the difference between being jealous, insecure, or someone actually cheating on you. Your gut instinct may be telling you that something is wrong, but you can't put your finger on exactly what it is, so look for signs. You may want to broach this subject, but beware that they may get frustrated or angry, and that doesn't mean they're guilty. It may simply mean they don't like being accused of something they haven't done. You don't have the right to look through their cell phone, purse, and wallet or read their journal. Those are all very personal and private, and you will only drive them away by doing so. You do have the ability to check their Myspace or Facebook since they are on public display and see who their friends are and what comments they are leaving, but don't read more into it than what is actually there. There are other means of looking into their life when you're not together, but spying is typically a one-way street. Once you begin, you will always be suspicious of what they do or where they go even if they're innocent. So either learn to trust them and believe they're making the right decisions when you are apart or end the relationship and find someone else that doesn't arouse your suspicions. If you find that this is a reoccurring problem in your relationships, then consider that the problem is you, not them. In this case, you need to seek counseling for your jealousy, insecurities, and trust issues before you enter into another relationship; otherwise, you are destined to repeat the past.

Jenifer

If you've been in several relationships and you always suspect people of cheating, you need to look at yourself and deal with whatever happened in your past to make you so cynical of everyone. On the other hand, if you have been in several relationships and you have never felt that the other person was cheating until now, there is a good chance your suspicions may be accurate. But consider this: even if your suspicions are not accurate, this is probably not the right person for you. Everyone brings something different out in each of us. The key is to find the person who brings out the best in you. If they bring out a side of you that is jealous and suspicious, you might want to consider moving on.

* * *

Women commonly say that men are not good communicators, and that's true because we are not telepathic.

Once you finally meet the person you want to be with, don't screw it up with poor communication. If something is bothering you, talk about it before it becomes bigger than it needs to be.

Mind Readers

Jim

How can we be expected to understand what women want if they don't tell us? If they only understood that we don't always know what is in our own minds, maybe they would better understand that it is impossible to know what's on theirs. If you detect that they're angry or frustrated and ask them if they're okay, they will invariably say that they're fine and then continue to pout until they work themselves into a frenzy because you didn't read their mind. When a man says he's fine, that's exactly what he means, so we don't understand when women don't say what they mean. Women commonly mention that men are not good communicators, and that's true because we are not telepathic. When this happens, try to bite your tongue because no matter how many times you tell her you don't read minds, she will still expect you to.

Jenifer

Oh boy, Jim, you're funny. I think there might be a little female bashing going on here. I have been with plenty of men who expected me to read their mind, so I think this is a two-way street. Let's just say communication is one **of the major keys to a successful relationship. Once you** finally meet the person you want to be with, don't screw it up with poor communication. If something is bothering you, talk about it before it becomes bigger than it needs to be. Most people will be very appreciative if you just sit down and discuss it respectfully. All this avoiding **and pretending is only frustrating to both parties and** ultimately damaging to the relationship, not to mention immature. When you are dating, look for someone who communicates well with you and someone you communicate well with in return. This will go a long way to **the future success of the relationship.**

*   *   *

They talk more than you can listen, and invariably, they either put their foot in their mouth or you stop listening.

When nerves get in the way, they can often make people talk too much or not talk enough.

Blabbermouths

Jim

The UCSF Woman's Mood and Hormone Clinic published a study called "The Female Brain," which states, among other things, that women speak an average of twenty thousand words per day compared to a mere seven thousand by men; since the numbers are almost three to one, I am directing this subject at the ladies although there are blabbermouth men out there too. Blabbermouths are women that just don't know when or how to shut up. They talk more than you can listen, and invariably, they either put their foot in their mouth or you stop listening. It's difficult to tactfully ask a woman to talk less, so hopefully they get the hint when you stop listening. However, some women take offense if you aren't paying attention to them, and if that's the case, tell them honestly that they're talking more than you can listen and that silence is a good thing sometimes. If they get upset or continue chattering incessantly, understand that this is just the way they are and decide if you can tolerate it. Conversation is when one person talks, then pauses so the other person can talk, so it's a give-and-take proposition. When one person does all the talking, it's a monologue, not a conversation; and it won't be long before you either can't take it anymore or you just stop listening.

Jenifer

I have to revert to good communications skills again. Blabbermouths don't have this skill, so they're difficult to date. You'll have to decide if you can deal with it or not. I love to talk and have great communication with someone, but I also enjoy silence and appreciate it when someone can enjoy it with me. However, silence makes some people nervous, so if a person talks too much or is too quiet on the first date, they may just be nervous. Once they get comfortable, they will probably talk less. Don't jump the gun too quickly on this one; go out enough times to see the real personality as you rarely get someone's real personality on the first or second date. I recommend you always give people the benefit of the doubt on this subject. At It's Just Lunch, we take feedback after each date, and this is one of the most common complaints we get about the other half of the date. I recommend that people go on the second date because this problem will probably take care of itself as the person relaxes. If the blabbermouth problem continues, I say you'll have to decide if it's something you can live with.

* * *

Wedding Ring or No-Pest Strip

Jim

I have only known this to happen with women, so I am addressing it as such. When you come across a woman that wears a ring on her wedding finger, it is not always a case of her being married; it may, in fact, be what is known as a no-pest strip. This usually means that the woman works in an environment where men are constantly hitting on her, and it's an easy out for her to appear as if she's married even though she may not be. The best way to find out is to simply ask. Should you find that she's married, respect the vows she made to another man and leave her alone.

Jenifer

I disagree with Jim on this one. If you come across a woman with a wedding ring on, she is wearing it for one reason only. She wants everyone to think she is married, including you. Don't bother asking; that's what she is trying to avoid in the first place.

* * *

Work on being their friend until their divorce is final and understand the rebound problems.

Divorce is scary, and many people feel alone when going through one; they get into relationships because they need support during this very difficult time. You may just be filling a needed role, and once the role is not needed anymore, your relationship could change drastically.

Separated People

Jim

Danger, danger, danger! There are different degrees of separation, but beginning a relationship with anyone that's not divorced isn't a good idea. Consider the risks beyond committing adultery; they may reconcile, their spouse may be angry and confront you, they will likely be jealous, and if they're in a house formerly shared, they may barge in on you, which could lead to violence, etc. The possibilities are many, and none of them will really end well for you. Work on being their friend until their divorce is final and understand the rebound problems.

Jenifer

I agree. There is a lot of danger here, but I also know that everyone's circumstance is different. Get the whole story, then decide if it's something you should get involved in. Honestly, I think the circumstance would have to be extreme before I would recommend becoming involved. If you do proceed forward, go very slow. When considering the circumstance, keep in mind that once most people are 100 percent sure they want a divorce, they file for one. Lots of people say they're not divorced because they cannot agree on how to split the assets, or they cannot agree on custody. The truth is, if you really want a divorce, you would file first, then argue over such matters in the divorce battle. If they haven't even filed for divorce, they may not be 100 percent sure they want one. The other thing one should consider is that going through an ugly divorce takes a toll on the relationship. New relationships can rarely withstand such a challenging event. One last thing to keep in mind: Divorce is scary and many people feel alone when going through one; they get in relationships because they need support during this very difficult time. You may just be filling a needed role, and once the role is not needed anymore, your relationship could change drastically. My advice would be to look for someone who is completely divorced, but if you give in and start dating someone going through a divorce, you need to move very slowly.

*   *   *

If you're dating a person you know is on the rebound, keep them at a distance and don't let yourself get too attached to them, and know that each time you see them could be the last.

The Rebound

Jim

This can be a roller-coaster situation with many ups and downs and usually ends in an abrupt halt. People that are going through this tend to have cycles of "come here, come here, come here," then unexpectedly "get away, get away, get away." One time, they'll say how much they enjoy you and want to spend every minute together, then they don't return your calls for a week. After a month or two of this, they abruptly disappear, and if they do call, it's for the old "it's not you, it's me" chat. So if you're dating a person you know is on the rebound, keep them at a distance and don't let yourself get too attached to them, and know that each time you see them could be the last.

Jenifer

I would give the same advice as I gave in with dating people who are not completely divorced. If you choose to date someone on the rebound, move very slowly.

Sometimes it works out and sometimes it doesn't, but either way, it is a very risky territory, and you risk getting hurt. Move slowly, take your time, and keep your eyes wide open!

* * *

Sugar Mammas

Jim

You are likely familiar with the term *sugar daddy*, so think of *sugar mamma* as the female equivalent. She has money and is willing to offer it to you in exchange for your company or more. Some of these women are really looking for a man they can keep and take care of in a live-in-type relationship. They'll insist that you don't work and offer to provide anything you desire along with an allowance. If you enter into this type of relationship, you'll have little control and will probably find yourself under the thumb of a controlling woman. Should you decide to exit the relationship and regain your independence, realize that you will be unemployed, with no income, and have little or no savings. What you've really done is prostitute yourself for a period of time with nothing to show for it but some nice clothes and maybe a decent car if you're lucky. Remember that if you stay with this type of woman, she may decide, at some point, to trade you in for a newer model, and you'll be lucky to receive a small severance if any. Enter at your own risk, understand what you're giving up, and accept the outcome.

Jenifer

My advice is always geared toward finding a long-term exclusive relationship. Sugar mammas and sugar daddies are not normally long-term relationships, so I will decline to give advice on this subject matter.

*   *   *

Cougars tend to enjoy young men like candy and want as many as they can get while they're still appealing, so don't be hurt if she tires of you after a short time and moves on.

Cougars

Many young men dream of older women. A cougar is an older woman that seeks the company of younger men. **Their youthfulness makes her feel more alive. Cougars are** disinterested in men their own age and seek men that are at least seven years younger. Men should understand that eventually she will probably find someone her own age as the young men interested in her dwindle over time. Cougars tend to enjoy young men like candy and want as many as they can get while they're still appealing, so don't **be hurt if she tires of you after a short time and moves on.** It's nothing personal; she's just enjoying what she wants at that point in her life. Accept it for what it is; don't be disappointed if she dumps you and rotates someone new **into your "bull pen."**

* * *

If you want to date attractive women who take care of themselves, a certain amount of maintenance goes along with this.

High-Maintenance Women

Jim

Spotting people that are high maintenance is usually not too difficult if you're in a place where you can hear them order something. When a woman goes to Starbucks and it takes her thirty seconds to rattle off her coffee order, then it doesn't take supreme deductive powers to know that she's probably like that in all aspects of her life. Typically, if they're at a restaurant, same deal. There is nothing wrong with them getting exactly what they want, but you can bet that if you get into a relationship with them, they will expect you to give them exactly what they want the way they want it, and if you don't, look out. They will make your life unhappy and twist it to seem as if it's your fault that they were so demanding. High-maintenance people **can also be manipulating and controlling. You have been** warned.

Jenifer

Okay, guys, this is the thing. When a women walks past you in a restaurant and she is dressed perfectly, with beautiful hair, just the right amount of makeup, etc., you turn your head and look twice. Well, guess what, it takes a certain amount of maintenance to look like that every day. When you guys come into my interview room and tell me what your physical appearance requirements are, you all ask for women who take care of themselves, women who look young, dress with style, look feminine, know how to throw on jeans for a hike or wear a sequin gown to the ball, and of course, you want someone who is physically fit and not too overweight. But if we go into Starbucks and order a fat-free, sugar-free latte, we are too much trouble? How do you suggest we maintain our weight if we can't order our coffee without fat and sugar? You want feminine, but are we high maintenance if we get our nails done? I suppose everyone has a different definition of what high maintenance is and a different tolerance level for it. I'm not sure I agree that high-maintenance women can be any more manipulative or controlling than low-maintenance women. All I'm saying is, if you want to date attractive women who take care of themselves, a certain amount of maintenance goes along with this. You'll need to decide how much is too much. My personal opinion is that if it takes her two hours to get ready before she can leave the house, it's probably too much.

*   *   *

They will see the bad side of everything and everybody.

You may want to think twice about dating a person who has a negative attitude toward life as they will not bring out the best in you.

Negative Attitudes

Jim

Negative people will eventually find a way to bring you down no matter how positive you are. They will see the **bad side of everything and everybody. Over time you may** find that they have slowly turned into someone you didn't want them to be. Like the "glass half-empty" person that mopes around and always suffers from the "poor me's." Spending time with them is a downward spiral and will **eventually have negative effects on you. They're likely** not worth the effort, so cut them loose and find someone positive.

Jenifer

Positive people bring you up, negative people bring you down. Earlier, we talked about meeting people who bring out the best in you. I seriously doubt a negative person will bring out the best in anyone. Meeting someone upbeat and positive is one of the things I get asked for every day in my business. If you want to go on second dates with people, it is imperative that you develop a positive attitude and show it when on a date. A lot of people get discouraged by dating and spend a lot of time on their dates talking negatively about dating. The people you are meeting on dates come out to have fun and get to know you; don't be a downer by talking about negative things. You may want to think twice about dating a person who has a negative attitude toward life as they will not bring out the best in you.

*   *   *

If they devote all their time to their children and only want to spend time with you when it's convenient for them, consider letting them find someone else as your time should be more valued than that.

People with Children

Jim

This is a personal preference and depends on if or how much you enjoy children and how old they are. If you really don't relate well to small children, then teenage children **may not be a problem. If their teenagers don't like you** or seem to control their parent, it will lead to difficulties when they see you entering the picture. If they devote all their time to their children and only want to spend time with you when it's convenient for them, consider letting **them find someone else as your time should be more** valued than that. However, it doesn't mean that they can't end up in your bull pen, which I will cover later. Make sure **you completely understand the complexities of dating** someone with children.

Jenifer

This subject is very complex and also extremely important. The reason the subject is so complex is because every person's situation is different. Some children have an involved parent, some have no parental involvement. Some parents have a lot of family support, and this allows them plenty of time for a relationship others may have very little or no support. Some children are attached to their parent's leg, others have been raised to be more independent. The examples could go on and on, but the point is that no two situations will be exactly the same. When we do interviews at It's Just Lunch, we find that most people put some parameters around dating people with children. Some people only want to date people with children while others only want to date people without children. Some don't want to date people with children under a certain age; others only want to date people who want to have children, and again, the list goes on and on. Think about this long and hard and keep in mind that no two situations will be the same. Don't decide not to date people with children because you did it once and it was difficult. Decide not to date people that don't want to have children if you are 100 percent sure you want to have a child. This is probably not a compromise you should make as it's highly likely to present serious problems in the future. As I said early in the book, ask yourself why you feel the way you do about this subject and decide if your reasons are legitimate; be reasonable but set limits that will work for you.

*   *   *

Keep them at a distance and never put yourself in an emotional situation where you couldn't walk away in ten seconds flat.

If you desire to find a long-term relationship, stop playing and get serious.

Dating a Player

Jim

Typically, people that are players are elusive with their time and only want to see you when it is convenient for them. They have their own bull pen, and you are simply in the rotation on occasion. The signs are usually the same for men and women. Here's an example: When you're out together and she notices every man in the place, don't be offended and remember that like you, she's always looking to improve the talent of her bull pen. Try to control your feelings and don't become involved; keep them at a distance and never put yourself in an emotional situation where you couldn't walk away in ten seconds flat. Enjoy it for what it is, which is simply dating, but protect yourself, and if you're intimate, practice safe sex.

Jenifer

Bottom line is, no one wants to date a player. If your goal is to move from one relationship to the next and always be playing the field, continue. However, if you desire to find a long-term relationship, stop playing and get serious. Please make sure your little man always wears his raincoat regardless whether you're dating a player or not. It's just the smart thing to do.

*   *   *

My advice is to stay clear of this situation; it will bring chaos and drama into your life, not to mention that it's a bad way to start off a new relationship.

Are Their Crazy Ex's Lurking About?

Jim

Danger, danger, danger. If they have a crazy ex, then either they made them that way or they chose them knowing they were already that way. This is a huge red flag. If they made them that way, then guess what, you're next. If the ex was already unstable when they first met and they didn't see the signs or chose to ignore them, it could prove to be a dangerous situation with a limited upside. When it comes to restraining orders, it's usually the woman that applies for one, so here is what men should watch out for: **Women that have an extended history of having judges place restraining orders on their ex's have usually missed the warning signs or are unstable. If she mentions that she has a restraining order on her ex, you may want to ask if she has ever had to do it before. If it sounds like common practice for her, then consider it a red flag. However, it should be understood that most restraining orders are** necessary, and the men that violate them should be locked up. There are women that abuse the system, and the minute the relationship ends, she claims the need for a protection order even when there is really no fear from the man. It's simply to be vindictive and stain the man's reputation and may also show up when he applies for certain licenses. Avoid the headache and don't ask for a second date.

Jenifer

We've all heard about or possibly experienced that person who seemed very normal for three months, six months, maybe even a year. Then all of the sudden, the signs start becoming clear, and the true colors begin to surface, and before you know it, you have a crazy ex on your hands. It doesn't have to be anyone's fault, but the reality is, a crazy ex is lingering. It is sad when this happens, but they need to deal with the crazy ex before entering into another relationship. My advice is to stay clear of this situation; it will bring chaos and drama into your life, not to mention that it's a bad way to start off a new relationship. Allow them time to deal with the crazy ex and revisit later.

*   *   *

Hold her gaze until she looks away because when you look away first, she associates it with running away and a lack of confidence.

If you're interested in getting to know someone better, tell them! Don't try to guess by their body language.

Body Language

Jim

This is a great resource when used properly, and I only recognize the signs a woman displays, so here we go. As mentioned before, it all begins with eye contact. Hold her gaze until she looks away because when you look away first, she associates it with running away and a lack of confidence. When making eye contact, notice her body position. If she glances your way and turns her back on you, then the body language is that of someone not interested, likewise if she is facing at an angle away from you with her arms folded in a defensive posture. However, if you make eye contact and she smiles back and adjusts her body to face you, then she's showing signs of interest that she may not even know about. If you recognize the signs and decide to approach her, don't be a "close talker" and make sure your breath is fresh. You only have about ten seconds to imprint your confidence on her, so keep her gaze and lean in slightly and don't touch her too soon. Many women have bad memories of men that were aggressive and all hands. That never works, so if it's something you've done in the past, don't do it anymore. When you approach her and she leans away from you, the signs are saying she's not really into you or that you're crowding her space. Back up a little and get **out of her space and see if her posture returns to normal** and proceed. If she turns away from you, then read the sign and don't take it personally. When a woman is really interested, she will hold your gaze; her pupils may even become dilated, and she will smile at you, play with her hair, lean in slightly in conversation, and possibly touch **your arm. You can learn more about body language at your local bookstore or library.**

Jenifer

I agree that body language can be a great resource when used properly. However, I must caution you, on a first date, most people are very nervous, and oftentimes, the body language is misread. Since we actually get feedback about every date we coordinate for our clients, I have learned just how many people misread body language. I tell my clients, if you're interested in getting to know someone better, tell them! Don't try to guess by their body language. In my experience, if you're guessing, you will be wrong most of the time.

*   *   *

Breast Piercing

Jim

This has gone on for ages but, until recently, didn't exactly have a unified name. It is not hugging, but rather when a woman is chatting with you and consciously presses **her breasts against you multiple times. It may be for her** arousal, but more often, she's trying to stir up your natural instincts to pursue her. When this happens, you can actually call her on it if done humorously, but be careful as you don't want to embarrass her in front of others.

Jenifer

When I first read this topic and Jim's response, I thought to myself, "Oh my, I've never heard of this before," then **immediately started thinking back over my life to see if I** could ever remember doing it. I'm not sure what to say on this topic, but I am sure about one thing. If this ever happens to you, never ever call her on it; it doesn't matter how humorous you go about it.

* * *

If you're shorter than her, you're already at a disadvantage, and although you may have a few dates with her, the feeling that you're not tall enough may eventually bubble to the surface and she will probably move on.

Most women prefer the man be at least two inches taller than her.

Tall Women

Jim

Many men that are attracted to taller women don't get it when she ignores their advances, so here's the deal: When a woman is five feet ten and you're five feet eight, there may already be a problem, then you put her in three—to four-inch heels and she's towering over you. Woman want to be with a man that makes them feel safe, and when in his arms, she likes to feel small and protected. If you're shorter than her, you're already at a disadvantage. Although you may have a few dates with her, the feeling **that you're not tall enough may eventually bubble to the** surface, and she will probably move on. Tall woman tend to have a slightly limited pool of men to draw from, just as many men prefer petite women, and the ones that are interested in the taller variety will have to be at least as tall as the woman for her to feel the way she desires. If you are a short man that loves tall women, more power to you; just know that you may have to work harder to find what you're seeking.

Jenifer

Women either feel very strongly about a man's height, or they don't care either way. In my profession, I've learned there isn't much middle ground here. Most women prefer the man to be at least two inches taller than they are. Keep in mind I said most women. If you are a man on the shorter side, consider that your presence can make you seem taller. Many women have told me that they will date **shorter men as long as they have a lot of presence.**

* * *

For many men, this is the most coveted player in the game.

I usually learn that what they really prefer is a slender woman.

Petite Women

Jim

For many men, this is the most coveted player in the game. There is something psychologically that draws the majority of men to petite women. It may be that a man wants to be able to place his arms around a woman and have her feel safe in his embrace. Whatever it is doesn't matter as much as knowing that she's the most highly sought-after type of woman, and the competition may be fierce. With this type of woman, larger men may run into difficulties for a couple of reasons. You may be just too large for her physically where just the thought of intimacy with you is painful for her, or she may simply have a personal preference for someone closer to her own size. Either way, don't fight this uphill battle; simply let her find what she wants and you do the same. If you insist on a petite woman, then know it's a numbers game, and you may have to approach many until you find one that matches you.

Jenifer

Throughout my interviews, I would say 60 percent of men tell me they prefer a petite women and about 40 percent say they prefer taller women. When I ask more questions about what their definition of petite is, I usually learn that what they really prefer is a slender woman. I've also **learned through many questions that if someone meets a** person they really connect with, an inch here or there or an extra ten pounds is not going to stand in the way. Try **not to get caught up to these types of things and look for the best overall package.**

*   *   *

My time is valuable and yours should be too, and the people that don't value it are selfish, period.

There is no faster way to screw up a first date than by showing up late.

When They Don't Value Your Time

Jim

My time is valuable and yours should be too, and the people that don't value it are selfish, period. If you have plans for dinner at 6:00 p.m. and they don't show up until 6:40 p.m. and haven't called, then don't be there when they arrive. When they call to ask where you are, remind them that your plans were at 6:00 p.m., not 6:40 p.m. and that your time is too valuable to waste sitting at a **restaurant alone. Everyone can be delayed from time to** time, but someone that understands and appreciates the value of your time will make every effort to be there or call if they're running late, which is the courteous thing to do. If they're always late for everything, then it's probably **their thinking that nobody's time is as important as theirs.** I'm not a proponent of playing games, but if you know they're always ten minutes late, then tell them to be there twenty minutes earlier than you plan on showing up and see how they feel having to wait for you. Odds are they won't like it and will better understand that you don't either. They may fall back into their old ways, so you must either accept it, correct it, or kick them to the curb.

Jenifer

This is one of my personal pet peeves. There is no faster way to screw up a first date than by showing up late. You never get a second chance to make a first impression and this is not the impression you want to make. I'm not sure who decided that being "fashionably late" was fashionable because to be honest with you, it is downright rude. Being late screams that you're being selfish among many other things. When dating, allow plenty of time to arrive on time; actually, you should plan to be ten minutes early so there is no chance of being late. Arriving early will allow you an opportunity to relax and get in the right frame of mind for your date, helping you make the impression you desire. When planning the time and place of the date, don't cut things too close, making sure you will have plenty of time to arrive without feeling rushed. Being on time and relaxed will go a long way in making the best impression possible.

*   *   *

Knowing When They're into You

It's really not that hard to tell when a person is into you enough to ask for a date because that is exactly what they will do, but there is a separation between the sexes here. Men are traditionally the aggressors, and they usually accept that role; however, women aren't as predictable. For the men out there, it's simple. Does she usually answer when you call, and if not, how long is it before she calls you back? If she's interested, more often than not you will receive a return call that same day if possible, but the next day for sure. However, if she makes you wait three or four days or doesn't call you back at all, then take it as a sign that talking to you is not on her list of priorities. If when you ask her out she never commits to a date, you can figure that she is keeping you on hold, hoping for a better offer and that you're simply someone on the periphery of her dating circle. Accept that she's not that interested and move on, and you might just find that her interest piques as soon as you're no longer interested in her. On the other hand, when it comes to women, some are passive, always waiting for the man to make the first move. Others are slightly aggressive and may ask a man out if they have met or spoken before. Some are moderately aggressive and will ask a man out if they are unsure of his making the first move; and lastly, there are the shark-in-the-waters women that know exactly what or who they want and don't waste much time circling. They want quick results and will do what is necessary to achieve them. Women should understand that many men have been told by other supposed dating experts not to call for at least five days, which is a complete mistake, but don't be surprised if they make it and certainly don't wait on them as you don't know if they will ever call. The same rules apply as stated earlier for the men; if you're not at the top of their priority list, then consider distancing yourself from them. They may send mixed signals, but remember that if they're wishy-washy early on, it will happen more frequently the longer you know them until everything unravels and you're frustrated, so cut your losses and leave them standing in the rain without an umbrella.

*   *   *

Tools

Many women are not comfortable giving you their phone number or even their business card. This is why men need to have cards available so they can give them to someone their interested in but may not have a real opportunity to engage in conversation.

While I don't agree with having personal business cards made up, I do agree that you should always have something to give a great prospect your phone number on.

Business Cards

Jim

I use the term *business* because it is universally understood, but what it really means is a card meant to convey information you wish to share with certain people. These can be vital for a man to not miss an opportunity, but it is typically one-sided. Many women are not comfortable giving you their phone number or even their business card. This is why men need to have cards available so they can give them to women they're interested in but may not have a real opportunity to engage in conversation. I have used this many times, and it occasionally works; however, if she doesn't call, then just figure she wasn't interested and move on. Business cards **don't have to be expensive and don't really have to contain** any business information, but they should have more than your name and number. Women notice quality, so I would **recommend spending a little extra time and money and** getting something nice. If you don't have business cards, then get some printed up with your name, phone number, e-mail address, and a little something about you that is charming, interesting, or funny; and they may even have your picture. It's your choice. Business cards are a tool, so **use them as such.**

Jenifer

If a man handed me a business card with only his personal information on it, I would definitely think he was a man on the prowl. I mean, seriously, does he walk around all **day handing out his business card that doesn't have any** business on it to every single woman he comes across? I say, hand out your business card if it is really a business **card. Do not go have personal business cards printed!** If you want her to know you are giving her the card for personal use, point out that your cell phone number is on the card, and she can feel free to call it anytime. If your cell is not on your card, then write your cell or home phone **number on the back. Tell her you'd love to get together for** coffee and ask her to give you a call with some dates that she would be available. While I don't agree with having personal business cards made up, I do agree that you should always have something to give a great prospect your phone number on. Keep something in your wallet or purse and even keep something in your car. Lots of women are not comfortable giving their phone number to strangers, so men need to be prepared.

*   *   *

*Good wingmen realize it is not about them
and will do everything in their power to see
you succeed.*

*The goal of the wingman is simply to get a
group of the opposite sex over to the table
where you're sitting, then create enough fun
for them to want to stay there.*

Wingmen

Jim

Although this term has *men* in it, the fact is that it applies
to men and women equally. Watching a good "wingman"
work their angle for your benefit can be a sight to behold.
For the wingman, there is no pressure because what
they're doing is not for their own benefit so they can relax
and work for you. Good wingmen realize it is not about
them and will do everything in their power to see you
succeed. However, many so-called wingmen are really on
the prowl for themselves, and although they say they're
working for you, they really only have their interests at
heart, and the results will not benefit you. Wingmen need
to remember that when they're successful, you will owe
them one, and when you constantly work at repaying each
other, then lots of dating opportunities come into your
life, and it becomes easier to build your bull pen. It's really

about helping each other, and if your wingman gets selfish, then call them on it. Never argue over someone you both desire; simply take turns with who gets the first pick, or ask the person you're both interested in to decide for you. There are too many single people to fight with your friends, so work together to achieve your goals.

Jenifer

I agree. The wingman (if you have a good one) can be a great benefit. Women do this; we just don't call each other wingmen. When I go out with my girlfriends, I usually play the wingman role. I guess that's because I'm a matchmaker, so it comes naturally to me. The goal of the wingman is simply to get a group of the opposite sex over to the table where you're sitting, then create enough fun for them to want to stay there. Once everyone is talking, laughing, and feeling relaxed, you will have the opportunity to see if anyone at the table piques your interest. If so, proceed with my advice from the business card section. Tell her you'd like to get to know her better, give her your phone number, and ask her to call you with some dates that she would be available to meet for coffee. Then offer to call her if she would be more comfortable with that. Always let her decide if she wants to call you or have you call her. Coffee is very nonthreatening; it is not a big commitment, and most people enjoy coffee and conversation. You will get a yes a lot more often if you choose something simple, like coffee, for the first meeting.

* * *

Bull pens

Jim

For those that don't know, bull pens are usually three to four people that you can date at any given time, and every single person not in a relationship should have one. Less than three is a little small, and more than four can be problematic. Like a baseball team, you should always be looking to upgrade your players so that you have the best talent available. Your players should also know there are other players on the team to create a healthy competition. You need to rotate them into your dating game regularly and keep a notebook that covers your different conversations and where you went with each of them. Confusing what you've said or where you went to the wrong person can be embarrassing to say the least. Don't be afraid to let someone leave your bull pen as you bring in new ones. Three to four is a good number so that you can give each of them the playing time they want. Understand that when you commit to an exclusive relationship with one, the bull pen has to go. Don't be a jerk, honor your exclusive commitment, and be a decent person.

Jenifer

I can honestly say I don't know a thing about this. It sounds like a lot of work to me. In fairness, I'll admit I see the **benefits to having a bull pen. If you are not in an exclusive** relationship, it is nice to have someone to go to dinner or the movies with. It is especially nice to have a date if you get invited to a party or an event that will be mostly couples. As a professional matchmaker, my job has always been to help people find an exclusive relationship, true companionship, not to help build a bull pen. Obviously, **that means I don't have a lot of professional experience** in this area, but my gut feeling tells me that if you have to keep a notepad to track what you are saying and doing, something is wrong with this picture. Maybe it would make more sense to fill your so-called bull pen with a group of friends (truly friends) that you can invite at any given moment to events and other things that you wouldn't feel **comfortable doing alone. I'm going to go out on a limb** here and even suggest that your bull pen should include members of both sexes.

*   *   *

Having a henhouse can be risky in a variety of ways, so think long and hard before deciding to walk down this path.

The Henhouse

Jim

As a bull pen is a collection of players that make up your dating pool, a henhouse is different in that these are people that you are intimate with. You need to know that many women will avoid a man that admits to sleeping with other women. They don't want to share you, and if they know you're sleeping around, they'll probably get rid of you or try to convince you to commit only to them. Having a henhouse can be risky in a variety of ways, so think long and hard before deciding to walk down this path. Should you decide this is what you want, then protect yourself and your partners at all times. Condoms are a must in this situation, so don't be a dumbass and always wrap your Johnson. It's best to be honest with them, and they can decide for themselves if they want to participate. Remember that once most women have been intimate with you, they assume that you're monogamous and may become very angry if they discover otherwise.

Jenifer

Well, I can see we are digressing. Okay, here is the thing
with the henhouse. Yes I'm sure there are women out
in the world that will be intimate with you knowing you
are intimate with others. I would be naive to think any
different. If you are looking for a long-term exclusive
relationship, I would strongly discourage you from creating
a henhouse and encourage you to spend your time
on something that will help you accomplish your goal.
However, if you really just want to date a lot of people,
then the key here is to be honest with everyone in your
henhouse. The goal has to be total honesty to minimize
the hurt or pain this could cause others. From a health
standpoint, this could be dangerous, so the other goal has
to be protection at all times, no matter what.

*   *   *

If you lie to them, the truth will reveal itself when you meet, and you will have ruined any possibility of moving farther.

The benefit is that it's inexpensive, simple to use, and anyone can become a member of an online dating site (I suppose this could be the drawback as well).

Internet Dating

Jim

This is a subject that has become wildly popular. It is an easy way to find people that you know are single in all shapes, sizes, and ages. If you're new to Internet dating, keep in mind what you see is not always what you get. At some point, you will be deceived, but march on if you are **so inclined.**

Meeting women over the Internet is really more like an interview and while you are conducting your interview, remember that they will be doing the same. During this process, you need to be asking more than just any **questions; you need the right questions so you'll get** you the answers you're really looking for. When asking **questions through e-mail or over the phone—such as** "When were your pictures taken?"—what you're really asking is, do you actually look the same? When you mention that their profile says their body is athletic and fit, you'll want to ask how often they work out. By doing this, you're setting yourself up to walk out when you meet them **if they've lied to you. The question "Have you been dating online long?"** really means, is there something wrong with you that drives people away? These are just a few of the questions you should consider. People that lie will usually lie about two things: their age and their weight. Make it clear before meeting them that you won't tolerate liars, so if they show up for a meeting and they're thirty pounds more than they said, don't stick around. Don't feel bad about it either because they lied, not you. When meeting them, if you find that they lied to you about something, you don't owe it to them to stick around for an hour; you can split with no regrets. This works both ways, so don't lie about your age or weight and use current pictures. Remember that if you lie to them, the truth will reveal itself when you meet in person, and you may have ruined any possibility of moving further. Meet in a public place, be on time, dress appropriately, and never schedule it to last more than an hour. If the magic is there, you can always stay later or plan a second date. There is a service with a Web site called Phone My Phone at www.phonemyphone. **com; here you can enter your phone number and tell** them when to call you. This can get you out of a date if you don't want to stay the whole hour. People tend to be visual to some degree, so if the person online doesn't have a picture posted, it's usually for a reason, so ask them to **e-mail one. Never give out your home address as you really** don't know the person yet, and it's not a great idea to tell them where you work since they could become fixated on you and show up at your job.

Jenifer

As with any dating service, there are benefits and drawbacks. The drawback to Internet dating is that it is very time consuming; it is not private. No one is making sure that the person is using an accurate picture, being honest about their profession, or that they're even divorced. The benefit is that it is inexpensive, simple to use, and anyone can become a member of an online dating site (I suppose this could be a drawback as well). I certainly know people who have had success using Internet dating sites, and I think different services appeal to different people for different reasons. If you have limited income and a lot of time on your hands, this might be the perfect proactive approach for you to meet people. Beware, doing your own screening could lead to a lot more meetings than you anticipated, therefore making the cost of Internet dating higher than it may appear at first. Depending on your lifestyle and your goals, you'll have to decide if this is the right service for you. If you decide to give Internet dating a try, never give your personal contact information to anyone prior to meeting them. Just trust me on this. Ask very specific questions during the e-mail exchange. Make sure you're always honest. The last thing you want is to meet someone you really like and then have to admit you were not honest on your profile. Aside from that, it is important to meet someone who is interested in you for who you really are. Yes, you want to put yourself in the best light possible on your profile, but it still needs to be honest. Obviously, don't lie about your height, weight, or age. In addition to that, don't make yourself sound more **outdoorsy and active than you really are. Be yourself** and be comfortable with who you are. You will have a much-better experience with those you do meet.

*   *   *

Writing a Profile

So you have decided to join the Internet dating movement but aren't really sure where to begin. To start, you need to decide which site you want to join. The next step is writing your profile. It will usually contain information about yourself, such as what you're seeking in a partner and something about your interests, likes, and dislikes. You'll be asked to provide pictures of yourself, which should be current. You should provide a few different pictures in a variety of locations. If you decide that posting pictures isn't for you, then realize that you're limiting your possibilities and will likely receive only a few people contacting you or responding to your advances. Before you throw together a profile, you should read other profiles and create a list of what (in your opinion) makes a well-written profile. Once you have this list, begin building your own using ideas from others, but not their content. Make your profile long enough to convey who you are but not so long they're bored before they finish it. Accurate pictures with a well-written profile can attract the attention of the person you seek just as well as deception can ruin even the best connection upon first meeting.

*   *   *

Many people forget that matchmaking is a two-way proposition and that while they are interviewing you, you too must be interviewing them.

The person of your dreams will not show up and knock on your door one day. Take charge and be proactive.

Dating Services

Jim

These businesses offer a legitimate opportunity to meet the type of people you desire through matchmaking. Depending on the service, there are multiple plans that cover an array of prices. Remember that if you are accepted into their service after screening, you have an obligation to convey your likes and dislikes after the date so they can match you more closely for your next date. Many people forget that matchmaking is a two-way proposition and that while they are interviewing you, you too must be interviewing them. If you are unsure as to which company is right for you, then ask for references. When you are comfortable that you have found the right service, remember that they are the professionals, so trust them to be just that and help guide them as to what you really want.

Jenifer

There are different types and levels of service that are available from personalized dating services. When checking out dating services in your area, there are a few questions you should ask. Do they interview each client? If the service is claiming to do matchmaking, you will want to know who is doing the matchmaking—a person or a computer? What criteria do they use when choosing a match? Once a match is chosen for you, will they coordinate the date for you? If they do not coordinate the date for you, does that mean they're going to give someone you've never met your personal contact information? Services that coordinate the date will normally call both parties and choose a time and place that works for both of you, then make the reservation under both of your first names. This way, no personal contact information is given unless you show up on the date and decide to give it yourself. The next one is very important. Ask them if they require you to call with feedback about your match after the date. Why is this important? If they don't require you to call with feedback, how effective could their matchmaking be? The feedback is what tells them what you like and don't like, what's working for you and what's not working. Matchmakers don't have crystal balls, and if they aren't communicating with you before and after each date, it's likely the success rate will be lower. If you're going to pay for a personalized service, make sure it's really personalized. One big misconception about dating services is that you have to be desperate to pay for a date. If you choose the right dating service, you will not be paying for a date, but rather for a highly personalized, discreet, professional service. This type of service often attracts very high level professionals because of the privacy and because professionals don't normally have enough time for Internet dating. They need all the screening done for them so they can just show up and have very little time invested in each meeting. After all, time is money, so even though you might pay more up front, it could save you a lot in the end. People pay for a lot of professional services in life, such as personal trainers, housekeepers, dry cleaners, etc. A dating service is not any different. If you want a better result, you could increase your odds by hiring a professional. Regardless of whether you choose Internet dating, social networks, joining clubs, or hiring a professional matchmaker, you have to be proactive about your dating life. The person of your dreams will not show up and knock on your door one day. Take charge and be proactive.

*   *   *

Singles Clubs and Cruises

Singles clubs are organizations dedicated to creating singles events that offer a variety of activities, such as fund-raisers, wine tasting, dances, cocktail parties, speed dating, and so on. They will often plan games designed to encourage mingling and social interaction. Coordinating and scheduling these events take time and usually require some type of fee, which may be per event, per month, or even per year. Some also charge an initial sign-up fee for processing your paperwork and entering you into their database. The downside of this type of club is that almost anyone can join; there is very little or no screening, and most of the same people show up at the events, so there's not much of an infusion of new participants. The upside is the price and usually little else; however, it really depends on the organizers and their commitment to creating the very best club they can. For people that live in large cities and are considering joining a singles club, examine what each club offers and choose accordingly. Remember that at these events, there is usually no security, and you have no idea who is participating, so keep yourself safe when leaving.

Singles cruises, on the other hand, offer many of the same types of events as singles clubs but combine them for an extended period of time, usually three to ten days in length. Cruises are obviously more expensive as you're incurring the expense of not only the cruise but also the traveling to the jumping-off point. Events of this nature are sometimes offered to specific age groups, so when researching these, be aware of that fact and keep in mind that if you're in your forties and prefer to meet someone in their twenties, a twenties to thirties cruise might leave you high and dry. Lastly, you are somewhat of a captive for the length of the cruise and should be careful about getting to close to someone too soon as they may want all your time for the remainder of the trip.

*   *   *

Booty calls are one person going over to the others place, having sex, and leaving.

Have some respect for yourself and the other person; skip the booty call and spend your time finding something meaningful.

Booty Calls

Jim

This can be a great way to have some adult fun; however, it can also be painful if one person wants a relationship and the other just wants casual meaningless sex. So be up front and honest about what it is and don't be afraid to talk about it. Booty calls usually only last until one of you finds something better or enters into a relationship. Dating and having sex with a person is not a booty call—that's dating with benefits. Booty calls are one person going over to the others place, having sex, and leaving. Not spending the night and having breakfast in the morning and leaving when the sex is done. Lay down the rules of engagement early on so you both have a clear understanding of how this game is played. Remember that you may not be their only booty call, so practice safe sex every time and know when to leave.

Jenifer

If you've been without a relationship so long that you have to resort to booty calls, I suggest you go back and read the section on dating services. Once you become truly proactive about meeting quality people and following the advice in this book, you will be getting first, second, and third dates. This will lead to a relationship soon enough. Booty calls are risky from a health standpoint and an emotional standpoint. So have some respect for yourself and the other person; skip the booty call and spend your time finding something meaningful.

*   *   *

It is almost impossible for a relationship not to change after there has been intimacy.

Friends with Benefits

Jim

This is when you have a friend and the two of you mutually decide to have sex on a casual basis without expectation. People enjoy a certain comfort level when they can have "no strings attached" sex with someone they trust. This situation can help "keep the rust off," so to speak, and provide you both with fun and relaxing adult enjoyment.

Jenifer

This is simply a quick way to lose a good friend. Now if you're friends with someone and you decide to start dating, that's different. Lots of relationships start from being friends and grow from there. However, if you are just using your friend to "keep the rust off" (as Jim puts it), you **are certainly risking the friendship. It is almost impossible for a relationship not to change after there has been** intimacy. I am going to repeat what I said in the "Booty Call" section. **If you are desperate enough to start using your friends for sex, you need to be more proactive about finding a relationship.**

*　*　*

Condoms

Jim

They are always a good idea if you want to prevent pregnancy. You can't always trust that her birth control is working properly, so protect yourself. More than just pregnancy prevention, you don't want to be a carrier of disease or viruses, so wrap the *schvantz* and get yourself checked yearly for STDs if you're sexually active. Some people are carriers without ever knowing they're infected. Don't be one of them.

Jenifer

What more could you possible say than "wrap your salami"?

* * *

Approaching

When to Approach

Jim

This one is tricky. You have to weigh a few factors. If she's alone, then great, but more often than not, she'll be with others—sometimes out with the girls, a group of friends/co-workers, or even on another date. Then there are other times when she may be at work or with her parents or children, so you can see how this takes some thought. When she's alone, the approach should be easy. But when she's with a group of women, you may prefer to get in and out, whether asking for her number or giving yours, you will be the topic of their conversation for the next few minutes after you leave, so you can expect to feel a little uncomfortable. If she's with a date, you should be watching for signs of physical contact. If they are touchy-feely, then set your sights on a different woman. If they aren't, then your best opportunity is when he uses the bathroom because, for all you know, it's her brother or just a friend. If he doesn't leave her side, then appreciate that she's already with someone else and don't embarrass them or yourself by approaching. When she's with her family, be cautious and strike up a conversation with one of her family members first and use that avenue to work your way to her. When with her children, be extra careful and know that older children are naturally protective and may not like you from the get-go. I recommend that you find a reason to talk to her and give her your card; if she's interested, then she can call you when the time is appropriate. You may also strike up a conversation with her, and if she appears to be interested, you may want to ask for her business card and find time to make a quick call to her, and at that time, you can ask for her personal phone number. When it is a business function, never ask in front of her boss but find a way to learn enough about her so that you can look her up at a later date.

Jenifer

Jim is right, this one is tricky. I say, you can do it anytime as long as you're respectful. You will have a lot more success if you don't try to second-guess every situation, and you'll be wrong 90 percent of the time anyway. If she is with another guy, they may or may not be romantically involved. The chances are probably fifty-fifty. Keep in mind that it is rude to approach a woman that is with another man. So even if they are not romantically involved, it will indicate that you have no manners. The polite thing to do would be to wait until they are separated for a moment, then ask the man. If he tells you they are relatives or just friends, proceed with the advice from the next section and approach the woman. If she is with girlfriends or family, again I say use the advice from the next section, "How to Approach," and go for it. What do you have to lose?

*   *   *

When approaching a woman be honest but also know she is more likely to be interested if you have an air of confidence and are relaxed.

Introduce yourself, apologize for interrupting, tell her you can see she is with her friends/family, but if she gets a free minute you'd love to talk to her; let her know where you are sitting, tell her it was nice to meet her and you hope to speak with her again.

How to Approach, Be Honest

Jim

When approaching a woman, be honest, but also know she is more likely to be interested if you have an air of confidence and are relaxed. Don't be stiff or uptight; just relax and remember that the worst that could happen is that she's not interested. Don't use pickup lines; although some are actually very funny and can be good icebreakers, they usually come off as rehearsed, making the woman think you say the same thing to all women. She wants originality and to think you have sincere intentions about getting to know who she really is. Begin by making eye contact with her a few times and hold it until she looks away. If you're with your friends and she's with hers, use something honest like, "I couldn't help but notice you and would really like to get to know you a little better, but since you're with your friends and I'm with mine, I would like to get your number so we can meet for coffee or lunch sometime and I may know more about you." Then see how she responds. Most women understand that it is difficult **for a man to approach and admire the cojones it takes to** do it. They appreciate the honest, confident, and sincere way you handle yourself. The inside secret from a man I knew was this, "Look at them like you love them more than **life itself and try to pour those emotions out through** your eyes. Talk to her with confidence and honesty but know it's the emotion in the eyes that draws her in." He went on to say his conversation with them was nothing special; it was all in the eyes. You may want to try it, but don't match your conversation to the way you're looking at her, **or you may scare her. One thing both sexes may overlook is the handshake. Your handshake should be firm and** confident, but not overpowering. If you're not sure, then **ask a friend to help you gauge the proper tension. Never** place the dead fish in their hand as it's a total turnoff, a sign of weakness and lack of confidence. This may mean practicing until you get it right, but as you practice, you are also getting to know new people and expanding your **conversational abilities.**

Jenifer

In my profession, women constantly ask me for men with presence and a lot of self-confidence. In this section, I will give you ideas that scream self-confidence. Personally, I can assure you that men are really bad at approaching, so if you take this advice to heart and use it, you will increase your odds significantly. So the person you want to meet is with friends or family, and you are in a restaurant, nightclub, etc. Approach, introduce yourself, apologize for interrupting, tell her you can see she is with her friends/family, but if she gets a free minute you'd love to talk to her; let her know where you are sitting. Tell her it was nice to meet her and you hope to speak with her again and leave. The important part of that was to exit. Do **not hang around unless she invites you to join them and** obviously wants you to. I can assure you that if she is not in a relationship and is the least bit interested, she will find her way to your table. Let's assume you are in a lounge, pub, nightclub, etc., and you see a woman that you would like to buy a drink for. Do not, under any circumstances, ask the waitress to deliver a drink to the table for you! Ask the waitress what the lady is drinking, order one, and walk over to her table with the waitress. Then introduce yourself, tell her you noticed her drink was getting low, so you asked the waitress to bring her a new one. Tell her you'd love to get to know her better and point out the spot where you are sitting. Tell her if she has a moment, you'd love to chat with her, give her your phone number, **and tell her if it isn't convenient for her tonight to give** you a call, then maybe the two of you can meet for coffee or a glass of wine sometime. Leave! Go back to your own table and let her make the next move. If you don't, it will **come across as desperate instead of self-confident. It is** important that you deliver the drink with the waitress because there are certain risks involved with accepting drinks from strangers, and women should never do this. Buying a woman a drink and delivering it to her table with the waitress indicates a lot of self-confidence for several reasons. You felt confident enough that she would like you to spend money on her before making sure. You were confident enough in yourself to walk up and introduce yourself in front of her friends. Then you were confident enough that she would respond to walk away. Even if she doesn't come to your table, she will leave that night thinking, "Wow, that guy had a lot of confidence," and she will be intrigued by you. Obviously, there are a hundred different scenarios on where you might meet someone and who she might be with; the key in approaching is to always be confident and considerate no matter when or where you are approaching.

*   *   *

Once you've decided to ask for the phone number, don't delay because the longer you wait, the more fear can creep in and destroy your confidence.

Closing the Deal, When and How to Ask for a **Phone Number**

Jim

Since it is usually men that ask for phone numbers, I have addressed it as such. **This is the single largest deterrent** for men. They just have trouble asking for the digits, and **it's actually painful for them. Their adrenaline begins to** pump, the butterflies in their stomach turn into bats; they **become terribly nervous and choke out something totally** lame. If this is you, begin by making it a point to strike up a short conversation with at least one woman a day that you don't know and build up your confidence. After a while, you will find chatting with women much easier, which leads you to be more relaxed and confident. So once you've decided to ask for the phone number, don't delay because the longer you wait, the more fear can creep in **and destroy your confidence. Remember that a phone** number is simply that, and if you don't ask, you will never **have a chance to succeed. She may decide not to give you** her number, but don't be offended; simply give her your card. If she calls you at some point in the future, then great, but if not, at least you took the shot. She may give you a fake number; if so, take it as a sign that she wasn't interested but didn't know how to tell you, so don't waste time thinking about it and move on. All she really did was eliminate herself from your potential dating pool, so you know not to waste time on her in the future. If you run into her again and she hasn't called you, don't confront her, ignore her; neither of you need to be uncomfortable just because she wasn't interested.

Jenifer

My best advice is when asking for their number, always offer something low-key, nonthreatening, and not a huge commitment. I almost always recommend coffee. You could say something like, "It was really great talking to you, and I'd like to get to know you better. Maybe we could get together for coffee sometime soon." If she says that would be nice, you could follow up with, "How would you like me to contact you?" Coffee is very low pressure, and it will lead into asking how you should contact her naturally. Then she has the option of giving you her cell phone number, work phone number, e-mail address, whatever she is comfortable with. You will get a lot more numbers if you keep all the pressure off. I completely agree with Jim about talking to women you don't know regularly so you are very comfortable with striking up a conversation at any time. Remember, confidence will be the key when closing the deal.

The only problem with giving your number instead of getting theirs is that you have not closed the deal, you have put it in her hands and given up all control of outcome.

Giving Your Number

Jim

As with the last subject, this is directed toward men. Be careful with this as your card may fall into unwanted hands, such as that of a jealous boyfriend or husband, so know that you may get an unexpected or unwanted call. This is rare but has happened. You may also find, to your dismay, that she has given your number to one of her less-than-attractive friends, and unfortunately, you may not discover the bait and switch until you're meeting in person. Ouch! When giving your card, keep it simple and easy by saying something like, "I would really like the opportunity to get to know you better, but I know that you may be uncomfortable giving me your phone number, so I would like to give you mine in the hopes that you'll call me sometime and we can get together for coffee or lunch." **Don't make it harder than it needs to be and stay** out of your own way by talking too much. Simple, to the point, and sincere. If she calls, then great; if not, you just **increased your odds that the next one may say yes.**

Jenifer

I do not recommend men simply offering their number.
I don't feel it shows confidence. If you feel more
comfortable with not directly asking for her number, you
could use my advice above, "It was really great talking
to you and I'd like to get to know you better. Maybe we
could meet for coffee sometime soon?" Then this time,
when she says, "That would be nice," you could respond
differently by giving her an option. You could say, "Would
you like me to contact you, or would you prefer that I give
you my number?" In this scenario, you don't give up your
confidence, but you do come across as considerate. The
only problem with giving your number instead of getting
hers is that you have not closed the deal; you have put it in
her hands and given up all control of the outcome. Every
scenario is different, and using a combination of these two
choices, depending on the situation, is probably your best
bet.

*   *   *

Ask questions, listen, ask more, and don't interrupt.

Relax and let your sense of humor shine through.

Calling Her the First Time

Jim

If calling a woman for the first time, spend a few minutes writing down questions that are thoughtful and encourage her to talk about herself. The worst thing is calling a woman and realizing you weren't prepared, and the call feels awkward with extended silences. Be interesting, which may mean spending a few minutes on the Internet to find out what is happening locally, nationally, and internationally. **Since this is the first call and you don't** know which direction it is going to take, prepare yourself to cover a wide range of topics. Remember that you should really be calling to learn about her, not to talk about yourself. So ask questions, listen, ask more, and don't interrupt. If the conversation begins to drag, be polite, end it, and let her know when you will be calling again. If all goes well, then set a time/place for the first date.

Jenifer

Early on in the book we talked about how being a good conversationalist is the key to being a good dater and ultimately getting second dates. The advice for the first introduction is very similar to the advice for calling her the first time. Everything Jim said is spot-on. You need to be a good conversationalist, be interested and interesting, be prepared to talk about things you know you have in common, and ask questions to find new things in common. Relax and let your sense of humor shine through. Don't stay on the phone too long. It is important to talk in person during the beginning stages of a possible new relationship. Call, chat a little, learn a few things, and plan your next date. Remember to laugh and make sure your conversation is upbeat and positive.

*   *   *

By ending it first, you have made a statement that you are confident and in control of yourself.

End the Phone Call First

Jim

There is an old show business saying, which is "Always leave them wanting more." This too applies to your first **phone call. Plan on keeping the call going for three to five** minutes, and early on, let them know that you only have a few minutes before you have to go. However, if you feel the chat waning or the conversation becoming disjointed, confirm when and where you are going to meet for your **date. Thank them for the brief chat and that you need to** be going and look forward to seeing them. On the other hand, should the conversation be easy and fun, let it last a little longer, but still, be the first to end it. By ending it first, **you have made a statement that you are confident and in** control of yourself. When either a man or a woman hang on to the conversation too long, they come off as clingy, which is undesirable. After you have chatted a few times and are comfortable on the phone, it doesn't really matter who ends the conversation first.

Jenifer

If the call is going well, I don't think it matters who ends it. However, if the conversation starts to drag or become strained, it is important that you say something to pick it back up and end the call very shortly after.

*   *   *

First Date

Be on time, dress appropriately, observe proper hygiene, have an idea of what questions you want to ask.

You are not going to see a person's real personality on the first date.

First Date

Jim

This is it. Make it or break it, so be on time, dress appropriately, observe proper hygiene, and have an idea of what questions you want to ask. Don't be cheap, but don't be extravagant either. She may talk a lot but know that she's probably nervous, so just ask questions and listen. Don't be a braggart, name-dropper, or blabbermouth. Remember that she wants to talk about herself, so don't interrupt and let her. Give her your undivided attention and watch how she treats the server or the comments she may make about others in the establishment. Is she kind or rude? After about an hour, think about wrapping it up. If at a restaurant, when the check arrives, pay the bill and leave at least a 20 percent tip. A woman may lose interest if you're a stiff, and she'll think you're cheap, so just spend a couple of extra bucks.

Jenifer

Having coordinated and listened to feedback from literally thousands of dates, I can tell you that many people make the same common mistakes. The biggest mistake is deciding too quickly if this is a person you want to go on a second date with. Let me just tell you, you are not going to see a person's real personality on the first date. You're not going to determine all the things you have in common on a first date. You're probably not even going to know exactly how much or how little you are attracted to them. Oftentimes people will become more attractive if they have a great personality. Since you probably aren't going to see the great personality among other things, it will be hard to determine the actual amount of physical attraction or chemistry. Now I know that a lot of the people reading this right now are disagreeing with me. Many people believe they will know in five minutes if the person sitting across the table is someone they would like to date. You're going to need to trust me on this. Unless you can tell me that you've talked to hundreds of people into going on second dates that they didn't want to go on, with people that they were sure they would not want to date, only to call and thank you profusely for talking them into it, then you will need to trust me. I know what you're thinking right now; you are different. Listen, you will increase your odds of success by 70 percent if you go on second dates with people. If you really want to meet someone and you could increase your odds by 70 percent, why in world wouldn't you? What do you have to lose? The second most common mistake is misreading the other person's body language, and even though you want to go on the second date, you don't ask for it because you think the other person is not interested. I cannot tell you how many people call us with feedback about their date, tell us how much they liked him or her, but they're sure the other person was not interested, so they didn't ask for the second date. Then the opposite person calls to tell us how much they liked them and how disappointed they are that no second date was planned. People are nervous on the first date, and everyone acts different when they're nervous. You really need to give people the benefit of the doubt, go on second and third dates, give them a chance to relax with you, and see what happens. If you're on the first date and you're interested in a second date, don't second-guess the situation. Tell them you are interested in seeing them again and getting to know them better. I know this is hard advice to follow, but try it. I don't think you'll be disappointed.

*   *   *

If he calls too soon, he comes across as clingy, and if he waits too long, the window of opportunity may be closed.

Calling within twenty-four hours is optimal, but calling within forty-eight hours is imperative.

When to Call Her Again

Jim

In most situations, it is the man that's expected to make the first call, so, men, here you go! Two common mistakes men make when they like the woman is either calling too soon or waiting too long. If he calls too soon, he comes across as clingy, and if he waits too long, the window of opportunity may be closed. It's really simple—call in a day or two but don't wait more than three, or she will likely lose interest. Men are told and believe that waiting five to seven days is effective in creating a burning desire for you; that opinion is bogus, and consider the fact that after three days, she assumes you're not interested anyway, and even when you now show interest, it's too late. You don't like waiting for the phone to ring, so don't expect her to wait on you.

Jenifer

I would recommend calling the next day and thanking her for the nice time you spent together. Confirm that you would like to see her again and start working on a day that will work for both of you. Calling within twenty-four hours is optimal, but calling within forty-eight hours is imperative. As I mentioned earlier in the book, women want to feel like you were taken by them. They want to feel like you can't wait to see them again. They also want to feel like you have a strong-enough personality to move things forward. You do want to make sure you don't come across as too pushy or desperate, so don't call several times a day, and don't keep calling if she doesn't return your phone call. Call once and leave a nice message by thanking her and asking her to call you back. If she does not call within two days, you should give her the benefit of the doubt and call one more time. If you do not hear back after the second message, do not call again.

* * *

How Much Do I Spend?

A typical first date for lunch should run $20-$35, depending where you live. A meeting for coffee is about a third of that. Never go for fast food; choose a decent sit-down restaurant, preferably a place that's not too noisy so you can have a conversation without straining to hear each other. One common mistake that men make is going to an extravagant dinner on a first date, spending a ridiculous amount of money, only to find out the woman just isn't interested in them. Don't do it. Save the extravagant dinner for something special when you know them better and already have a strong connection, not when you're still figuring out if you even like each other.

* * *

I would recommend that the man always offer to pay. I know it's not fair, but reality is, most women still appreciate traditional gentlemen qualities.

When Should I Pay?

Jim

The standard is, if you invite them out, then you pay; if they invite you, then expect them to pay; if you want to go Dutch, then let them know before you meet. If they insist on paying their own way, then let them. Their refusal to let you pay may be a hint that they aren't into you, so don't fight it. No matter what, always bring enough money to cover your own meal.

Is she taking advantage? (Again, it's usually the man that has asked the woman out on the date, so this is directed at the men.) It depends on what she orders. If she orders a couple of appetizers, a large lunch with dessert and an expensive glass of wine, then yes, she probably is. If it's soup, salad, and an ice tea, then you should be okay with it. Remember that you can learn much by watching what and how she orders, especially if she thinks you're paying.

Jenifer

I would recommend that the man always offer to pay. I know it's not fair, but reality is, most women still appreciate traditional gentlemen qualities. Opening the door and paying the bill will go a long way in making a good impression. If she insists on paying, then definitely let her. About 90 percent of women tell me they are impressed when the man pays for the date. The other 10 percent prefer to pay for themselves, and in this case, you should respect that.

*   *   *

You already know everything about yourself but probably almost nothing about them, so ask, then listen and don't interrupt.

It is important that you let them talk about themselves and that you ask questions so they know you are truly interested.

Ask Then Listen, Listen, Listen, Then Ask More

Jim

This is an easy one. Most men want to talk about themselves, and women are no different, so you need to set up a situation where they're able to do just that. Besides, you already know everything about yourself but probably almost nothing about them, so ask, then listen and don't interrupt. You will find that as they give you more information, you'll have more questions to ask, so let them lead. When this happens, you'll find that they **become more interested in you because you are really** listening. So pay attention to what they say, and when you have questions, ask. This is where many people go wrong. They begin talking about themselves, and before you know it, an hour goes by; they blabbed incessantly you feel like your hairs on fire, and you can't wait to get away. If there comes a point when they want to know about you, they'll ask. So keep your own storytelling short and turn the subject back to them. Focus on what they're saying, comment appropriately, and move the questions forward.

Jenifer

I think two-way conversation is the best bet. It is important that you let them talk about themselves and that you ask questions so they know you are truly interested. It is also important that they learn some things about you so they will know if they want to go on the next date. Jim is definitely right about blabbing incessantly. This is a complaint I receive often, so I know many people make this mistake. You will not get second dates if you don't have a good two-way conversations and if you are not truly listening and interested in what the other person is saying.

*   *   *

Forgotten Introductions

Jim

While out on your date for lunch or coffee, someone from your past walks up to your table and says, "Great to see you again." You look up to recognize the face and have no idea what their name is. As you fumble through a short conversation with them, the tension builds as your date is wondering why you haven't introduced them yet. Eventually they introduce themselves, and the visitor does the same. You continue the chat briefly, and the person leaves. This has happened to everyone at some point, but make sure to explain to your date that you didn't introduce them because you had forgotten the visitor's name and didn't want to embarrass them. You should also tell them that if a similar situation ever arises again, you would appreciate their help in doing the same thing so the name comes out. This will assure them that you're not trying to hide them from your friends, which would usually be their first assumption.

Jenifer

This happens to people all the time, and it's embarrassing to everyone involved. If you handle it the way Jim suggested, your date is sure to understand.

*   *   *

Choose a place that encourages conversation and has a good atmosphere, show up on time, wear your new date outfit so you feel like a million bucks.

Good Dates

Jim

A fun mutual experience is not necessarily a place or an event, but the way the two of you interact. However, if you don't separate yourself from the competition that may also want their time, you may get lost in the shuffle. Most people have first-date failures because they either fail to ask questions, talk about themselves too much, or are just plain cheap. If you asked them out face-to-face, then there's already some attraction, but if this was a blind date or setup on the Internet, it's all about the initial chemistry. So go there feeling great with your energy level in control and make the conversation fun. Never do a movie for a first date. If you go to a movie, how are you going to let them tell you about themselves? Consider somewhere they can have your undivided attention, and save the street festival or concert for another time.

Jenifer

All through the book we've been telling you how to have good dates. Half the battle is being proactive so that you get dates. Let's recap on how to have a good date once you've got one. Choose a place that encourages conversation and has a good atmosphere. Show up on time, wear your new date outfit so you feel like a million bucks, be interested and interesting. Keep the conversation upbeat and positive, never talk about your previous dates, your ex's, or negative things going on in your life, and have enough self-confidence to ask for the second date. It really is that simple!

*   *   *

I truly believe that one of the biggest mistakes single people make is trying to decide in five minutes if they are attracted to someone.

Attraction

Jim

When a man's attracted to a woman, he knows it immediately. As visual creatures, we are driven by what we see, and although some women deny it, they are much the same. Within five minutes of meeting, a woman has already decided if she wants a second date. As long as you don't act like a pig, things should move forward rapidly. The difficulty arrives when only one person is attracted. If she is attracted, then that's an easy call for you to make, **depending on your end goal. If you're looking for casual** meaningless sex, then you can probably get it at the risk of hurting her feelings. If you truly want a long-term relationship, move on and find a woman that you have a real chemistry with. If you're the one attracted, then accept it if she turns you down for another date. If she's someone that you seem to run into regularly, consider working your game more slowly and making an effort to get to know her and become friends. Women are auditory, **and although the initial physical attraction may not be** there for her, it is possible to work your way into her heart with your words and gestures. If this is how you're forced to approach her, know that it's a difficult path that may not lead where you want. If you still want to go through with it, then do the little things for her. Offer to help with something small like picking up an item at the store, taking her to the airport, or buying her a small bauble to remind her that she's in your thoughts. *Don't overdo it.* Don't crowd her or become clingy; simply attempt to be her friend. More than one man has achieved the woman of his desires by becoming friends first.

Jenifer

I'm not sure how you figure that if she is attracted to you, you can probably get meaningless sex, but I'm going to let that one go. Let's just say that attraction is a funny thing. You can know someone for years and never be attracted to them, then all of a sudden one day, they become attractive. I truly believe that one of the biggest mistakes single people make is trying to decide in five minutes if they are attracted to someone. Having coordinated tens of thousands of dates for people, I can honestly say that you will increase your odds of meeting the right person by 70 percent if you go on second dates. I highly caution you against showing up for a date and deciding very quickly if there will be a second date. Around 70 percent is a huge increase in odds! If you are serious about wanting a relationship, take my advice and go on second dates—a lot of them.

When you are together, your personalities bring out the best in each other and totally complement each other.

Chemistry

Jim

It begins with attraction, but goes far beyond. The attraction is magical although elusive, feeling almost euphoric, but that soaring high can be followed by a cavernous low. Coming down when the high fades can be painful and frustrating. However, this high doesn't always fade, and if you're lucky enough to share this amazing feeling for a lifetime, then more power to you. If you have chemistry with someone and decide to move into a relationship, don't forget that as with all relationships, there is maintenance that's required to keep that excitement. So be the person she can't get out of her head and do little things to remind her that she is important in your life. Most people like surprise weekend getaways, or send gifts to her work at unexpected times so they can be the envy of others in their office or prepare breakfast in bed "just because." Think along those lines and remember not to take them for granted just because they're yours now. Be the person that all their friends wish they had in their lives.

Jenifer

Chemistry is elusive and complicated. Everyone has their definition. I believe you've found chemistry when you've known a person for a few weeks, but it feels like you've known them a lifetime. When you are together, your **personalities bring out the best in each other and totally** complement each other. Look at it this way: When you take a chemistry class, you put two solutions together and hope to get a positive outcome. In relationships, you should look for the same result you would look for in a chemistry class. Unfortunately, people look for chemistry in the first fifteen minutes the same way they look for attraction, and as a result, lots of good matches are tossed aside because **someone didn't take the time necessary to finish the class.** This is not a race, and you shouldn't be speed dating. Chemistry and physical attraction do not always show up immediately and will often show up as you are getting to know a person.

*   *   *

Don't Act like a Player

During your date, give her your undivided attention. When you look at every woman that walks past, she'll know she doesn't have your full attention and will label you a player or, worse, a womanizer. Women in their twenties actually like the challenges of dating a player, but women a little **older have already travelled that road and usually still** have the emotional bumps and bruises. If you show signs of being a player, they'll avoid you like the plague. If this is your first date and you're attracted to her, give her the respect of your attention. Don't talk about other women you may be dating unless she asks, but if she does, be honest and brief. Avoid discussing any past relationships, and remember you are there to learn about her, so act **accordingly.**

*   *   *

Equality Versus Old-Fashioned

Jim

Each of these qualities may be what women want at any given time, but it's always at her discretion, and there's no finite line as to when she wants to be treated a certain way. Women want to be treated as equals but will also tell you that they're old-fashioned. If they wanted complete equality, they would open their own doors and regularly pay for your meals, but some women hide behind the veil of old-fashionedness because it suits their wants at the time. This is difficult for men to understand because we are not mind readers, so if you're not sure what she expects, then ask her.

Jenifer

The reason men have such a hard time understanding this is because equality and old-fashioned traditional gestures are two completely different things. Once men learn to separate them, they won't need to be confused. Just because we fought for the right to vote or own property does not mean we don't want the door opened for us. Opening the door for a woman is a sign of respect and has nothing to do with equality. Not all women agree with me, but this is my take on equality. Men and women are equals but simply play different roles in society (example: women have babies and men don't, men are normally bigger and stronger than women), this doesn't make one sex any better than the other; it just makes us different. Obviously, women want to be treated as equal citizens, but this does not mean that we think we are exactly like men or that we play the same exact role in society. Old-fashioned gentlemen qualities are something completely different and still show a sign of respect and caring toward women. In my profession, about 90 percent of women say they appreciate men who have gentleman qualities, and only about 10 percent say they find it demeaning. I agree with Jim; if you're not sure, ask her.

Tip: for those of us who appreciate it, the gestures will go a long way.

*   *   *

After an hour or so, you can ask her if she has other commitments or if she would like to continue the date.

Ending the Date

Jim

It's not always easy to know exactly when to end the date, but it is usually based on what you did. For something simple like coffee or lunch after an hour is considered the norm. If you are inclined to ask her out again, then let her know that you enjoyed her company and would like more of it. A woman will usually say she would enjoy that even when she wouldn't just so she can avoid hurting your feelings or any potential for a conflict. You'll know her intentions when you call. If she doesn't return your calls or even tells you that the chemistry was missing, don't let it bother you and simply find someone else.

Jenifer

As long as you're both enjoying the date, stay on it. After an hour or so, you can ask her if she has other commitments or if she would like to continue the date. If she has only planned for coffee or lunch, she may have made a prior commitment. If this is the case, then see if you can set up a time for the second date and let her go to her prior commitment. If she has additional time, then take advantage of the opportunity to get to know each other better. Remember, this is your first date, so choose things that allow for conversation and good interaction. A walk along the river after your coffee or lunch can be a great chance for you to chat without distraction.

* * *

Second Date

The fact that you put some thought into the date will go a long way in getting the third date.

Second Date

Jim

Okay, you made it past the first date and did well enough to make it to a second, so again, you need to ask questions, let them respond, and begin telling them a little about yourself (a little means just that). At this point, hopefully they've realized that all they did was talk **about themselves on your last date and should be more** interested in learning about you. As before, you need to give them your undivided attention and show your interest in what they have to say. This time, though, you may be doing something like dinner and a movie or play, maybe even some live music. For men, don't try to impress her with something extravagant or overly expensive. Keep the dinner to around $40 with whatever comes after around $40. Remember that this date is not just about her, so you **need to be having fun also.**

Jenifer

For the second date, I would again suggest a setting that allows for ample conversation. The first three dates are very important, and choosing the right venue can make or break the date. If it is wintertime, dinner is the most obvious choice, but if you want to do something out of the box, you may choose to take her to a cooking class. Cooking classes are fun, interactive, and social. A play or a concert would also be a good idea, but not quite as interactive as a cooking class. If you choose one of the latter, make sure you do something quiet before or after so that you get a chance to talk and connect. If your second date is during nice weather, I would suggest a picnic at a nearby park or lake, followed by a nice walk or trip to the closest gourmet ice cream shop to share a banana split. The point I'm trying to make here is, don't just do the standard dinner and a movie. The fact that you put some thought into the date will go a long way in getting the third date. Again, keep it light and fun, but make it a little more romantic than the first date, making sure to choose a venue that will allow you to continue to get to know each other.

*   *   *

When to Kiss

Jim

If you didn't kiss her on the first date, then this should be the one. Some women prefer to wait until the third date, but the second is better for a couple of reasons. If it's the end of the second date and she still isn't willing to give you a kiss, then the third date will probably be the same, so why waste time or the money? Second, it's not like you would be the first man she has ever kissed on the second date, which says that she was willing to do it with someone else, not just you. Remember that a kiss doesn't mean sticking your tongue down her throat, so if that's your thing, then save it for another time. It's not always easy to tell if your date is receptive, so sometimes, you just have to go for it and see what happens. The end of the date is the usual time to make your move. If she lingers before leaving, she's giving you your shot. However, if she attempts to make a quick exit, then don't bother trying for a kiss and certainly don't ask her out again. Women don't want to be asked if it's okay to kiss her; they consider it a lack of confidence or that maybe you're a wuss, so go for the gentle kiss. If she turns her head so you kiss her cheek, then don't ask her out again and find someone that's more interested in you. If she decides not to kiss you, don't take it personally and move on.

Jenifer

I have mixed feelings about this one. I do agree with what Jim said, but I also know from my experience of dealing with so many different people, all in different places in their life and with different upbringings and experiences, that I'm not sure it's as simple as Jim puts it. I agree that it is probably a good indication that the person may not be interested in you if they don't want to kiss you after the second date, but then again, maybe you didn't do a very good job of making them feel comfortable with you. I'm not sure it's fair to say that a woman should be comfortable enough to kiss every man that she has spent approximately three hours with. I think you have to take into consideration where the other person is in their life, how many hours have you actually spent together, if you already knew her before your first date, or if you were a total stranger. I think it would be more important to determine if her behavior is telling you she is interested in you. Yes, kissing is one way to determine this, but there are many other ways as well. If you are interested in her and getting any indication that she is interested in you, I say give her the benefit of the doubt and ask her out again. It is hard to find the right person, so going the extra mile with each person will only increase your odds of success.

* * *

Men need to know that women warm up slowly and should be treated as such.

Kissing is a very intimate and romantic act if you treat it as such; the other person should respond positively.

How to Kiss

Jim

It's wise to begin gently and increase the passion as the situation calls for it. If you begin too aggressively, then you may miss out on any further activity. Men need to know that women warm up slowly and should be treated as such. Keep your lips soft and wait until she slips you the tongue before reciprocating. Don't stick your tongue down her throat, go slowly, and understand that you may need to kiss differently with different women. Some women want soft gentle kisses while others may prefer wet and sloppy, and still others may have an active tongue, so just go with it. If you are not sure what is pleasant for her, then ask. This will also let her know that you are more interested in what she enjoys. Should you find a woman that's not a good kisser, be very careful about coaching her as she may take it personally, and nobody wants to hear that they're a lousy kisser. If the woman suggests some changes in your kissing, listen to her and adjust your technique accordingly.

Jenifer

I think it's really important to start slow and see how the other person responds. It's no doubt how comfortable you are with each other and how much time you've spent together combined with the amount of natural chemistry will determine how this kiss will turn out. *Warning:* **Just because a person responds well to your kisses does not mean she wants you to push further. Kissing is a very intimate and romantic act if you treat it as such; the other person should respond positively. Don't be overly aggressive and don't push your limits. Pay close attention to how the other person is responding and proceed accordingly.**

* * *

If you treat it as a race, you'll remain single.

It's Not a Race

Jim

Although you may be aroused, remember that women warm slowly, and it's the foreplay that sets the tone. If you're racing through to get laid, you may find yourself alone with your hand rather than the woman you could have had only a short while earlier had you been patient. At some point in the past, men had been termed as an octopus as they were all hands, and the women had to **defend their advances. Don't be that guy. When things** are getting steamy, it's okay to make advances, but if she moves your hand away, accept that she isn't ready yet. It's not to say she won't be more inclined in the future as long as you don't rush her. This shouldn't need to be said, but there are always some dumbass guys, so *no means no*, end of story.

Jenifer

Same as the first kiss, everyone is in a different place in life with different experiences and backgrounds. It's not **a race! It's about finding someone that you can have a** successful long-term relationship with. If you treat it as a race, you'll remain single. When you meet someone you like, take your time, be respectful of where they are in the dating dance. Take plenty of time to get to know each other and to be truly comfortable with each other before crossing into intimacy. Trust me when I say, intimacy too soon has ruined many relationships.

*   *   *

Touching

Jim

Start with something simple like placing your hand on her knee, shoulder, or hand. If she pulls away, then take it as a sign that she isn't ready for physical contact yet or simply isn't interested a physical relationship with you. Look for the signs; is she enjoying your advances? This is what men hope for, and it may be as subtle as touching your hand, arm, or shoulder, but the main thing is that she is interested enough to touch you. Touching your hand doesn't include a handshake; however, placing her hand on the back of your hand, leaning into you, or placing her arm around you are more direct signs that she's interested. Read these signs for what they are, but don't read more into them than what's there.

Jenifer

Simple touching is always the best place to start—putting a hand on the knee, reaching for her hand as you're walking, etc. Her response should be telling and will give you a good indication of how she will respond to that first kiss. Beware, not everyone is comfortable with public displays of affection. If she is not responding, wait until you are in a more private atmosphere and try again.

When it comes to massaging, Jenifer and I both agree that crossing into someone's personal space is a delicate proposition and should be done when certain of her interest. Don't get grabby with someone you don't know. Keep your hands to yourself until you know she's interested in having you place them on her. You should learn about massage and the areas that produce the best effects if you're inexperienced. Take your time and remember it's about her, not you.

*   *   *

Everyone moves at a different pace, and all relationships progress differently. What has worked for your last relationship may not work for this one.

Crossing into Intimacy

Jim

Most women understand that the third date is the tipping point for many men. However, if you're both ready and know it's what you want, then go for it. The warning is that sometimes things change after the sex is over; for instance, they may expect monogamy from that point forward, they may become a cling-on (clingy) or even angry if you don't want to spend the night together. For men, the first intimate encounter should be at her place, if at all possible, for a couple of reasons. First, you have more control and can get up and leave anytime; and second, if she ends up being a stalker, you don't want her to know where you live, plus you don't have to worry about her leaving things at your place that will give her a reason to come by again. Don't take her to your place until you're sure you want her there, and don't be afraid to tell her when she needs to go **home.**

Jenifer

Call me old-fashioned, but if you are really worried about not wanting to spend the night, being able to get up and leave anytime, or her being a stalker, you probably shouldn't be having sex with her. Maybe you should slow down and get to know her better before proceeding forward. As I said earlier, being intimate too early in a **relationship has ended many relationships that may** have worked. Everyone moves at a different pace, and all relationships progress differently. What worked for your last relationship may not work for this one. You should not be crossing into intimacy until you are comfortable with each other and know where the relationship is going. You should definitely talk about what the expectations will **be after the sex is over to make sure you're both on the same page. The reason intimacy causes so many problems is because people don't bother to have this conversation up front. You have to decide if you're looking for sex or a** relationship. If you're looking for a relationship, be mature and considerate enough to talk about what is comfortable for both of you. **If you are one of those guys that expects** sex by the third date, you might find yourself single for a long time.

*   *   *

Third Date

The main thing is to spend a longer period of time together and see if you are actually compatible.

Third Date

Jim

If you made it this far, things should be pretty good. Hopefully you've already kissed, and it was pleasant for you both. This date is usually the dropping point, so if you get to a fourth, then you're onto something. You should be **more relaxed and both of you feeling a level of comfort. If** you have not been intimate yet, then this is a good date for some private time. Ideally, the date would be an all-day event—maybe hiking or biking somewhere in your area, followed by making dinner together and maybe a glass of wine or two and see where it goes. If you have been intimate already, a weekend getaway may be in order, **even camping if it's something you both enjoy. The main thing is to spend a longer period of time together and see if you really are compatible. This is the date to completely** be yourself. It's also their last big test for you. If you pass, then it should become easier, but if you fail to measure up to what they want, ask them if they can tell you where you **failed so you can try not to make the same mistakes in the future. Listen to their advice and move on.**

Jenifer

The third date is a great time to plan a romantic dinner at home. This is the make-or-break date, so be sure to plan something that encourages a lot of alone time so you can get into more in-depth conversations and share some romance as well. Cooking dinner together is fun and romantic; being completely alone together will encourage both of you to be yourself and engage in different types of conversation and behavior than you would in public. By now you are probably thinking "When is it a good time to see a movie?" I would never recommend a movie for the first, second, or third date. If you like the movies a lot, I would recommend waiting until the fourth or fifth date. By the end of the third date, you should know for sure if this is a person you want to have a fourth date with. Prior to the third date, you may not be sure how you feel about the other person. Look at it this way. The first date is simply to see if there will be a second date. The second date is to relax and get to know each other better. Most people are so nervous on the first date you don't see the real personality. On the second date, you are sure to get a little closer as to who they really are. By the end of the third date, you have seen a more relaxed person and had enough conversation to determine if you have similar goals, interests, and sets of values. If you make it to the fourth date, you are probably onto something interesting. When people don't follow through to the third date, they often give up on the possibility before they have any idea if this is a good fit for them.

*   *   *

It comes down to four things—attraction, chemistry, timing, and desire.

Are You Connecting?

Jim

Sounds like this should be pretty easy to figure out, but it's really not as easy as you think. It comes down to four things—attraction, chemistry, timing, and desire. Attraction and chemistry have already been covered, so **timing and desire are next. Timing and desire mean that you should both desire the same type of relationship at the same time. If you are looking strictly to date multiple** people and they want more of a committed relationship, then the timing of your desires don't coincide; therefore, **you need to move on. Both people must want the same thing at the same time for anything serious to get off the** ground. If it's not there, then don't try to force it, and don't lie to get what you want. If you're an honest person, **you may just find that the timing works for the two of you later on in life or that they have friends to introduce you** to.

Jenifer

It is more complicated than it sounds. Timing is a huge part of success in the dating dance. I would highly suggest having a conversation about what type of relationship **each of you is looking for on the second or third date. This**

is why I never suggest going to the movies early on. You don't want to go on ten dates with someone just to find out that you are at completely different places in your life or that your value systems are completely opposite. As we said, keep the first date light and fun; on the second date, go a little deeper in the conversations. Since the third date will be longer and more private, talk about long-term goals, what you are looking for in a relationship, etc. By the end of the third date, you should know if you're connecting on many levels.

*   *   *

The standard rule of who pays is this: whoever does the inviting does the paying.

Does She Ever Volunteer To Pay?

Jim

Women who believe in equality should not always expect you to pay for everything. The standard rule of who pays is this: whoever does the inviting does the paying. If you invite her somewhere, expect to pick up the tab. If she invites you, then she pays, and if you're going Dutch, then discuss it before the date. This is not being cheap, but practical. Many men have been flattered when a woman **asks them out on a date to a fancy restaurant but end up** disappointed that they get stuck with the bill at the end of the night. So if she invites you out, drop a subtle hint that you appreciate her wanting to pick up the tab and would **be happy to join her and thank her for the invitation. You** will find that this weeds out the women that expect you to always pay, and besides, who always wants to pay for everything? It's nice having someone treat you from time to time.

Jenifer

I've had men tell me that a woman will never pay while on a date with them no matter what! Then instruct me not to send them out with women who will have a problem with this. Like Jim, other men feel that they shouldn't always have to pay. I don't think we have a hard and fast rule here. I think it would be best to learn how your date feels about such things and go from there. I do agree that it's nice to have someone treat you from time to time. If you are a woman and you find yourself dating a man who always offers to pay, make a point to take him out to a nice dinner from time to time. Have cookies delivered to his office, plan a picnic with a nice bottle of wine, etc. It is important to show appreciation and to do nice things in return.

* * *

It may take more than one meeting with your friends before everyone is comfortable, so don't get too concerned if the first meeting isn't perfect.

Is It Time to Meet Your Friends?

Jim

On a third date, probably not unless you accidently run into them. The third date should really be just about the two of you in a private setting. The fourth date or beyond is really a more appropriate time to meet your friends. Remember that after they do meet your friends, your friends will have opinions and insights as to what they thought about the new person in your life. So listen to them as they may see warning signs that you don't. Now when it comes to meeting their friends, be confident and don't be afraid to interject into the conversation. Avoid being clingy and too quiet, and as always, be educated and compliment their friends, asking questions that allow them to talk about themselves or subjects they are knowledgeable about. If the conversation turns to politics or religion, tread lightly until you know if you're like-minded; if not, keep your opinions to yourself at this early stage of getting to know their friends.

Jenifer

Definitely not until after the third date, but meeting your friends is important. This is a good opportunity to see how they fit in with your circle. It may take more than one meeting with your friends before everyone is comfortable, so don't get too concerned if the first meeting isn't perfect.

*   *   *

Walk the line of not too quiet and not a chatterbox.

Double Dating

Jim

Not for a third date but possibly a fourth and beyond. You may want them to meet your friends, and you may want to do double-date things together, but this is just too soon. When you do double-date with your friends, make sure you **give them plenty of attention and encourage them to participate in the conversation. People can be** shy meeting someone new, so understand that they may be **quiet early on but should open up later. If double dating** with their friends, join in the conversation, but don't talk too much. When people are nervous, they tend to chatter like monkeys, so don't let that happen to you and don't interrupt. Walk **the line of being not too quiet and not a chatterbox.**

Jenifer

I think a double date with one of your closer friends is a good idea after the third date. This would be easier than bringing someone new into a whole crowd of friends all at once. The double date would allow for getting to know one or two friends at a time and would probably be more **comfortable for everyone involved.**

What Do You Really Want Now That You're Getting to Know Them?

Jim

Now that you have had two or three dates and known them a little better, are your thoughts still in line with what you wanted originally? You may find that your plan was simply to have another player in the bull pen, but now **you're interested in more or maybe the reverse. The really important part is that your timing and desires match. You** may even find that one of you has lost interest, and if that's the case, let them go or accept that they have let you go. Don't be one of those people that want them even more now that they're not into you. Be careful when you have discussions about your relational desires; you don't want to scare them away by wanting too much too soon. Although communicating is good, there is also a time when you need to just shut up no matter how bad you want to let it out.

Jenifer

Now it's time to go back to the list we suggested you create in the beginning of this book. Remember? The one where you determined what your preferences and deal breakers are. Now that you're getting to know her, you **need to decide if she meets the criteria you originally set.** Make sure you are not overlooking the things that were important to you. If you overlook these things now, they will surely come back to haunt you later.

* * *

The title of girlfriend is only appropriate after you've had the exclusivity chat and are both on the same page.

Introducing Her

When introducing her early on, always introduce her as your friend followed by her name. Occasionally, men make the mistake of introducing her as their girlfriend or even jokingly as their future ex-wife. That's always a bad idea, and you may find yourself trying to climb out of that hole for sometime if you haven't completely buried yourself. The title of girlfriend is only appropriate after you've had the exclusivity chat and are both on the same page. Keep it simple and always be polite.

*   *   *

It is confusing to have people coming in and out of their lives and homes all the time, so make sure your new friend is a keeper before you make this move.

Introducing Family and Children

Jim

Don't rush into meeting their family as this could be trial by fire, meaning that it may be tense and unpleasant. **Parents are naturally protective of their children and** rightly so, but their brothers and sisters may be equally critical of you, if not more, so take your time, and don't **meet their family until you're ready. The same should be** considered when wanting them to meet yours; wait until they're comfortable with the idea.

For children, this is a case-by-case situation that only the parent can decide. If you're meeting their children, present yourself as someone that could become their friend, not another parent. In all likelihood, they don't want another parent, and by becoming their friend, it will be more natural for them to accept you. Remember, though, that **they are still children and may do or say things you aren't** expecting or you don't like, so wear your thick skin. They may also be very protective or jealous of you wanting to share their parent's time, so don't be surprised if they don't like you from the beginning, especially if they're teenagers. This isn't a book on parenting, so if it is you introducing them to your children, do your best, and if you need help, find other single parents and ask them how they handle it.

Jenifer

Don't rush this. Date a person for a while before you introduce them to your children. I recommend waiting until you have decided to date exclusively at a bare minimum. What is the point of introducing someone to your children if you haven't even decided to move the relationship to a boyfriend/girlfriend stage. It is confusing for children to have people coming in and out of their lives and homes all the time, so make sure your new friend is a keeper before you make this move.

*   *   *

Fourth Date and Beyond

You should be getting comfortable around each other, so you can start to ask more personal questions.

Fourth Date

Jim

So you've gone through with three dates and they're still interested; you have passed their tests, and you're beginning to think there may be something special about this person. By now you should know if they conflict with anything on your nonnegotiable list and have hopefully not seen too many red flags. This is not the point to let your guard down. Many people don't display warning signs early on, but they do pop up over time, so continue to keep your eyes open. This applies to you too; they will be watching, so continue to do the right things and be a good person. If you can't be yourself and still be a good person, then get some counseling until you can, and let this poor person off your hook so they can find someone who's in line with their desires.

Jenifer

If you get to the fourth date, you are definitely heading toward a relationship. The first three dates are to determine if this is a person you want to start dating. **The fourth date usually means your dating! Congratulate yourself but keep in mind that you still have a lot to learn about each other. You can go to the movies now but continue to plan dates that encourage talking and learning more about each other. The two of you should be getting comfortable around each other so you can start to ask more personal questions if you feel like; it is something you need to know about.**

*   *   *

If this is a good relationship, you certainly should be able to talk and decide if you are both willing to be exclusive.

Exclusivity

Jim

This does not exist until the two of you have discussed it and have mutually agreed. If you're thinking about bringing it up, then think long and hard before you do because if they don't feel that way too, you may be left feeling disappointed that leads to the eventual demise of your friendship. If they bring it up and it's what you were hoping for, then great, but if not, be honest and let them know how you do feel. If you just want to be a serial dater, then tell them, but above all, *be honest*. There is honor in an honest person.

Jenifer

As Jim said, this has to be discussed. Too many people make assumptions and never really have the conversation. Be wise and discuss it. Assumptions lead to misunderstandings, and misunderstandings lead to problems, which ultimately lead to hurt feelings. Communication is the key to any good relationship. If this is a good relationship, you certainly should be able to talk and decide if you are both willing to be exclusive.

To be healthy, you need friends outside of your relationship, and friendships require time together to maintain them, so get out and do what's necessary.

Carefully consider everything your friends tell you and ask them questions about what they are seeing and feeling.

Listening to Your Friends

Jim

This is an asset that many people overlook or simply choose to ignore. Your friends have taken the time to build and maintain a friendship with you, so trust them when they make a comment on a person you're dating or involved with. If they tell you they seem controlling, abusive, or just plain not your type, listen to them and genuinely consider what they're telling you. This doesn't mean you necessarily do what they advise, but if they are giving you warnings, then listen up. If your friends tell you that you never get together anymore, think about why that is. Is the person you're seeing keeping you from them? If so, address the problem and get your life back. To be healthy, you need friends outside of your relationship. Friendships require time together to maintain them, so get out and do what's necessary. Remember, your friends were there before her and will probably be there long after she's gone.

Jenifer

Listen to your friends, but remember you know what works for you and what doesn't. This may be different from what works for your friends. Your friend may tell you **this is not the guy or girl for you because it's not the type** of person they are looking to be with. On the flip side, people looking from the outside of your relationship will often see things you can't see while in the middle of the **relationship. Carefully consider everything your friends tell** you and ask them questions about what they are seeing and feeling. You'll need to determine what's legitimate or **not.**

*   *   *

It can wreck relationships and families and destroys lives.

The emotion is so ugly and unhealthy it is not usually tolerated by happy, healthy people.

Fighting Your Jealousy

Jim

It's an ugly trait that can become a hideous beast when a person loses control. It can wreck relationships and **families and destroys lives. People have even gone as far** as killing someone over jealousy. In its heavier form, it can make seemingly normal minds twisted and dangerous, so if you have jealousy issues, then get counseling immediately **and don't get into a relationship until you have it under** control. Here is the issue with most normal men. If you are in an exclusive relationship and never show even a hint of jealousy, she will begin to feel that you don't care about her, but on the other hand, if you are overly jealous, she will think there is something wrong with you and probably leave. It's a fine line that constantly moves, so you need to keep it in check and reassure the woman that you care without acting stupidly. If you are dealing with a person that is extremely jealous, suggest that they seek counseling. At some point, they could become dangerous to themselves and others, including you, so if they begin to become emotionally unstable, document everything and contact the police. People may damage property when their jealousy gets out of control, and speaking of control, don't get put into a position of them controlling you as they're jealousy grows.

Jenifer

Jealousy is one of the ugliest emotions I can think of. If you are the type of person that gets jealous easily, it probably stems from lack of self-esteem. You will need to work through the reasons you become jealous before dating. If the goal is to meet the right person for a long-term exclusive relationship, jealousy will be prohibitive. The emotion is so ugly and unhealthy it is not usually tolerated by happy, healthy people. If you don't address this and get a grip on it, one of two things will happen: You will either attract other unhealthy people into your life or your relationships will keep ending. Neither is the result you're looking for, so confront the behavior and deal with it before moving on.

*   *   *

Beginning Sexual Encounters

This is more about taking your time and knowing that **both of you are at a comfortable pace.** If you rush her into something she's not comfortable with, you will not only turn her off but also possibly frighten her. Remember, stop means just that, and no is no, so respect her boundaries. However, if the two of you are on the same page, then go for it. There are a few simple things to remember—don't shove your tongue down her throat, no hickeys, save the biting or hair pulling for a later date if that's what you both enjoy, and don't manhandle her breasts. It is better to begin gently, ask her what she likes, then focus on pleasing her. By doing everything you can to give her pleasure, you will likely get the opportunity to enjoy each other again. Hot, steamy wild sex can be fun too, but it is usually better when you know your partner better.

*   *   *

Pregnancy, Ouch!

Jim

Wear a condom every time, always, no exceptions. When men are carefree about wrapping their boinker, then they're not only exposing themselves to possible STDs but also the possibility of her getting pregnant. If you do get her pregnant, your decision making goes out the window. It's her body, and she gets to make every decision about it and whether to have the baby or not. Should she decide to have it, you're looking at making monthly child support payments every month for the next eighteen years; that's 216 payments and even if you only have to pay $400 a month, that's still $86,400, and odds are that you will be paying substantially more. Throw in the facts that the woman you impregnated is probably not your future wife; you'll now be bonded together for the rest of your lives whether you like her or not and that you're now a single father. Doesn't sound so great, does it?

Jenifer

Once again, Jim says it all. Taking chances is not fair to anyone involved. Not you, your partner, or the baby that will eventually be born due to carelessness.

*   *   *

How to Address Their Unexpected Behavior

You won't see it coming, then—*pow*—they do something completely off the wall, making you wonder what just happened. Many times it will be alcohol induced, but other times it will just be a hidden part of who they are. It may be something they do physically or verbally, but consider that it will likely happen at some point in the future. If it's physical, it could be something as gentle as suddenly crying for no apparent reason or as violent as punching someone in the face. The crying you could probably deal with, but it's a decision you have to make for yourself. The verbal could be as ugly as using their sharp poisoned tongue on a waiter or as embarrassing as dropping multiple f-bombs at a dinner with your parents. Only you can decide what's tolerable, but when you don't like what they've done, call them on it privately and let them know it is not an acceptable behavior. If they don't stop or can't control themselves, then dump them. It's that simple.

*   *   *

The key to disagreeing with someone is in how you communicate it.

Disagreements are bound to happen, so when you're choosing a partner, make sure you choose someone you can communicate well with.

Disagreements

Jim

It's impossible to agree with someone about everything. People have their own opinions that are formed by the sum total of their life experiences. The key to disagreeing with someone is in how you communicate it. Are you willing to compromise if necessary, and is the other person willing to do the same? It's okay to agree to disagree, but if that's the direction you're going in, then drop the subject immediately. Some people say that they agree to disagree but can't let the subject lie and before you know, it's escalated into an argument. So after you agree, let it go.

Jenifer

The key to any good relationship is communication. When choosing a partner, pay special attention to how the two of you communicate. When you have a disagreement, do you talk through it like two mature adults, or does it turn into an argument? As mature adults, you should be able to talk through just about anything, so if you find yourself in a relationship where the two of you are constantly arguing, there are a few things you should consider. One or both of you have poor communication skills. The two of you have good communications skills separately, but you don't communicate well together. Disagreements are bound to happen, so when you're choosing a partner, make sure you choose someone you can communicate well with and someone who has the ability to talk through a **disagreement.**

*   *   *

*If both of you (key word **both**) are not working on the relationship, then get into reality.*

When to Leave

Jim

When you have more bad times together than good, it's probably time to leave. If you've tried to work it out, but it just doesn't get better, then end it. It will be painful but liberating; you will second-guess your decision for months to come, and when you see them, all those emotions will be stirred up again, but be strong and move on.

Jenifer

Leave when you know the relationship is over. Many people stay because, in some cases, it's easier or more convenient. Many people stay because they claim they want to try to work it out. Are you both really working on the relationship? If the answer is yes, then you have a legitimate claim. If both of you (key word *both*) **are not** working on the relationship, then get into reality.

* * *

They were someone that you wanted to have a relationship with in the past, so they now deserve that respect.

How to Leave

Jim

If you're living together, then I recommend leaving when they're not there simply to avoid conflicts. Emotions will be running high, and they will likely be angry or scared that you're going or possibly happy to see you go, but either way, verbal conflict can ensue, and you want to avoid that. If, however, you aren't living together you should meet in a public place and speak to them as an adult and simply be honest. They were someone that you wanted to have a relationship with in the past, so they now deserve that respect. Remember that people typically need closure, so give them that satisfaction and move on.

Jenifer

Once you have spoken with your partner about your desire to end the relationship, the two of you should have a conversation about when and how to end it in a mature fashion. If you're experiencing too much anger from the other person to accomplish this, then I agree with what Jim said.

The Yo-Yo Game

Jim

This is a common problem that almost everyone has experienced and can be difficult to get a handle on.
You're in a relationship, but for some reason or another, things just aren't working out for one or both of you, so you break up. Then after a couple of days, you miss each other and decide to have a talk, and before you know it, the two of you are back in the sack. It works for a little while, but the same old problems are there, so you break up again. This breakup seems like it's going to last, then you run into them when you're out, and a freight train of emotions runs you over, which is amplified if they're on a date. Then you feel this "gut ache," and your brain kicks into overdrive, and you can't stop thinking about **them. Those feelings tend to override your memory of** the problems the two of you had, so you call them again, and from here, it typically goes back and forth for a while until you just decide it's not worth the pain and let it go. The yo-yo game is pretty hard to avoid, so it's just better to recognize it for what it is, accept that it may happen to you, and instead of pining away about your breakup, work on building a new bull pen.

Jenifer

The yo-yo game happens because even after the relationship ends, there is often a lot of emotions and leftover feelings for each other. Try to avoid this as it is usually painful for both of you. If it does happen and you can't seem to control it, you'll need to realize that the relationship is not completely over. It will end when one or both of you is completely ready for it to end.

*   *   *

It's a waste of time, and although you may still have feelings for the person, you should be looking forward in your life not reliving the past.

Ex's Are Ex's for a Reason

Jim

There is something that occurs occasionally when a married couple breaks up, and somewhere down the road, they decide to get married again. It doesn't work and usually doesn't last even half as long as the first time they were married. This also happens in relationships with the same results. Ex's are ex's for a reason, and whatever the problem was the first time will come back even more quickly in the second go-around. The reality is that it's a waste of time, and although you may still have feelings for the person, you should be looking forward in your life not reliving the past.

Jenifer

Truth is that sometimes it seems easier to get back together with your ex than to find and start a new relationship. You're thinking to yourself, "Well, at least I know exactly what I'm getting." That's right, and after that thought comes to mind, your next thought should be that what you are getting didn't work for you the last time. Sometimes it is simply that the timing wasn't right the first time. If that is the case and if it ended friendly without hard feelings, you may be able to try again. If the relationship originally ended because it was lacking something that one of you needed or because you didn't communicate well together or maybe it ended because of a lie or indiscretion, you should beware of trying again as the odds are really stacked against you.

*   *   *

If the relationship lasts past the three-month mark, it will probably start to heat up fast and begin to get more serious.

How Long until You Know It's Real

Jim

The general consensus is that somewhere between three and seven months is when people tend to fall in love. So if you know that you are someone that falls in love after three months of a committed relationship, then you better be looking for any and all warning signs between the two—and three-month mark. Even if you think you're in love, don't say it to them until you hear them say it first. Again, don't say it first, and if you don't feel it, then never say it. The l-word can be a dangerous beast, and once you let it out, you can't take it back, so be careful with it.

Jenifer

The first three months are normally a lot of discovery. If the relationship lasts past the three-month mark, it will probably start to heat up fast and begin to get more serious. It can take up to six months and sometimes even a year to really know a person, so even though it's getting serious, be on the lookout for red flags and changes in behavior. I don't think it matters who says I love you first; just make sure the other person is ready to hear it, or you may scare them off. How long until you know it's for real? That will depend on many things, and the amount of time is different for each person and each relationship.

*   *   *

True love is long-lasting and certainly doesn't come and go; it needs to develop over time. If you are in the right relationship, the love will continue to deepen the longer you are together.

Love at First Sight

Jim

When a man sees a woman for the first time and has an overwhelming desire to be with her, it's caused by some uncontrolled brain activity that the man wasn't expecting, and although he may think it's love, more than likely it's a case of desire combined with lust. The physical attraction is what we're drawn to, and our human nature as men makes us want to mate with her. It is not that love at first sight doesn't exist, but it is extremely rare, and you would be lucky if you felt it once in your life, and then it only really matters if the woman feels the same. Consider the odds that the woman you just met really is exactly what you're seeking for a partner in life and accept it for the desire and lust it is.

Jenifer

I am and always have been a hopeful romantic, but I don't believe in love at first sight. True love is something real and something deep. True love is long-lasting and certainly doesn't come and go; it needs to develop over time. If you are in the right relationship, the love will continue to deepen the longer you are together. If you are in the wrong relationship, you will grow away from each other or, as some people say, fall out of love. I'm not sure I agree with falling out of love, but that's a whole different conversation.

*   *   *

Are you enough alike to share commonalities, yet different enough to learn from each other?

Make sure they don't have any of your deal breakers and have the majority of your preferences.

Catch and Release or a Keeper?

Jim

Only you can decide this, and if you're leaning toward release, then you probably should release and let them move on. The keeper, on the other hand, may very well change your life and not always for the better, so enter into it with your eyes open and your heart closed until you are sure they're what you want in all facets. Consider the list of what you want in life and compare them to it. Can you both compromise and share a common direction? Are you stronger together than you were apart? Do you both want the same level of commitment? Are you enough alike to share commonalities, yet different enough to learn from each other? They don't have to be perfect in every way, but they do have to be what you really want in your life.

Jenifer

The questions Jim asked are perfect. You should also look back at the original list we suggested you make, the one with your preferences and deal breakers. Make sure they don't have any of your deal breakers and have the majority of your preferences. Ask yourself one last question: do you bring out the best in each other? If the answer is yes, you might just have yourself a keeper.

*   *   *

Ending It

This is never an easy thing to do, and don't be surprised if she becomes angry at first, then hurt, and eventually cries. The way you should go about ending it will vary depending on the length of time you were together, your level of commitment, and why you're ending it. If you **never had the discussion about exclusivity and you have** both been dating other people, then it may be something **as simple as not calling her anymore. If she calls you and** wants to know what's going on, then tell her that you need to talk, meet her at a public place, and give her a brief explanation why you are ending it. Don't let her lay a guilt trip on you; just tell her it didn't work out and be on your way. However, if you've been in a committed relationship over a period of time and need to end it, then be gentle and remember that it should always be done face-to-face. You owe it to her. Although it's uncomfortable to do, you should be honest and direct and genuinely empathize with her. While you're talking with her, remember a time in your past when someone dumped you and treat her the way you would want to be treated. You may even want to use the old "It's not you, it's me" and explain why you need to move on. Her emotions will likely come to the surface, so **be prepared to face them. If you do it correctly and truly** do care about how she feels, you may get the benefit of staying friends with her, which has the potential of her **introducing you to her friends at some point in the future.**

If they were really good to you but it just didn't work out, then make an effort at being friends.

When to Stay Friends

Jim

Just as you don't want everyone as your friend, you certainly don't want every ex as your friend. If your ex is bitter or a little unstable or maybe just flat-out crazy, then sever all ties. However, if they were really good to you but it just didn't work out, then make an effort at being friends. **Consider that they may have no interest in remaining your friend, and if that's the case, let them go and be cordial if you run into them. There is no real** downside to having them as your friend; however, if they become difficult, then end the friendship, but in being your friend, they have the potential of becoming your best wingman ever. Many people underestimate the value of an ex that's a good friend, so consider them an asset in meeting someone new.

Jenifer

I have changed my mind on this over the years. I used to be of the mind-set that if the person was good enough to fall in love with, they certainly should be good enough to stay friends with. Now that I'm older and have remained friends with almost every person I've been in a serious relationship with, I've changed my mind. Of course, I think **you should end every serious relationship in an** appropriate and courteous way and always be polite when you run into them after the breakup. However, being friends would imply that you still talk regularly and even possibly hang out together (as you would with your other friends). This can cause several problems. First and foremost, it will take the person who didn't want **the breakup a lot longer to get over it if they are still** communicating with you. Watching you move on with your life firsthand could be very painful. Second, regular communication will increase the odds of the yo-yo game **happening and even possibly a reconciliation at some** point, which will probably lead to another break up. Third, the two of you remaining in contact will be difficult for your future relationships to deal with. I'm not saying you should never stay friends with anyone you've dated, but keep these things in mind as it might not be worth it.

*   *   *

Conclusion

We've laid it all out there for you, and now it's up to you to take the guidelines contained in these pages and put them to use in your dating life. Although we have been the ones to tell you what to expect, how to act, and what to do when exposed to new situations, this book is not about us; it's about you, and it is a tool to help you achieve your dating desires. These pages have years of dating experience and knowledge within them, and if you really are interested in changing the direction of your dating life, you will incorporate our recommendations and watch your life evolve.

This book is only as powerful as your desire to change. If you read it and don't act on the information, you have wasted your time. Get off your butt, get motivated, get out of your comfort zone, and begin making things happen. Understand that rejection is normal and will happen, but think of it as an opportunity to find the right person that much sooner. If you're only really into serial dating, then be honest with yourself from the start. Don't lead people on with false hopes of a relationship. Be honest in your words as well as your deeds to attract what you want into your life. I guess what it really comes down to is this: "Be a good person, be a kind person, be an honest person."

About the Authors

Jim Ghiglieri is a former casino bartender in Reno, Nevada, and currently owns a computer IT business, Vertical Web Solutions, and is the CEO of Pirate Crawl LLC. Being unmarried and having avoided committed relationships most of his adult life, Jim became a serial dater. The situation came about due to his married co-workers continually commenting that he had the perfect life as a single bartender, dating different women all the time, so eventually, he believed it and stayed single. His experience as a player and his job as a bartender allowed him to watch what worked for other men and emulated it to some extent. Having been on hundreds of dates allowed him to hone his skills and therefore share his experiences with you here in this book. If you wish to have him cover other dating subjects, e-mail him at jim@whenplanetscollide.com.

Jenifer Rose. At the time this book was published, Jenifer was the owner of It's Just Lunch in Reno, Nevada, host of *The Plush Life* television show on CBS, as well as the host of a one-hour radio show dedicated to dating and relationships called *Skirted Issues with Jen*. It's Just Lunch is a dating service that caters to professionals using personalized matchmaking services. Jenifer has conducted thousands of interviews with singles interested in joining her service and has coordinated and listened to feedback from over twenty thousand dates. Jenifer has also held many dating seminars in an effort to help people find love in their life. Amazed by the high percentage of people making very basic mistakes while on dates and the inability to cover all the necessary information in one seminar, she realized the need for a book such as this one. Jenifer has been a personal matchmaker and dating service business owner for years and is a true expert in her field. In these pages you will read some of her best advice.

Edwards Brothers,Inc!
Thorofare, NJ 08086
02 July, 2010
BA2010183